Teddy Bears

Teddy Bears

Barbara Werkmäster
Eva-Lena Bengtsson
Per Peterson

Translated from the Swedish by
Joan Tate
American Advisory Editor, Joan Roberts

BARRON'S
New York • London • Toronto • Sydney

First English language edition published in 1988 by Barron's Educational Series, Inc.

Copyright© Barbro Werkmäster, Eva-Lena Bengtsson, Per Peterson, and Författarförlaget, Sweden, 1987

Copyright © English translation by Joan Tate, 1988

Published by arrangement with the Monica Norberg Agency.

The title of the Swedish edition is *Nallebjörnen.*

All inquiries should be addressed to:
Barron's Educational Series, Inc.
250 Wireless Boulevard
Hauppauge, New York 11788

International Standard Book No. 0-8120-5960-3 (regular binding)
0-8120-5955-7 (deluxe binding)

Library of Congress Catalog Card No. 88-22231

Library of Congress Cataloging-in-Publication Data
Werkmäster, Barbro, 1932-
Teddy bears.

Translation of: Nallebjörnen.
Bibliography
1. Teddy bears.   I. Bengtsson, Eva-Lena.
II. Peterson, Per.   III. Title.

GV1220.7.W4713   1988   688.724   88-22231
ISBN 0-8120-5955-7 (deluxe binding); 0-8120-5960-3 (regular binding)

Illustrations from *The Bear and Henry,* by Arlene Blanchard, Barrons, 1987. Illustrations copyright © Jean Claverie, 1987.

Text and illustration from *Enter T.R.,* by Terrance Dicks, Barrons, 1988. Text copyright © Terrance Dicks, 1985; illustrations © Susan Hellard, 1985.

Illustration from *Doctor Squash and the Doll Doctor* by Margaret Wise Brown, illustrated by J.P. Miller. © 1952, Western Publishing Co., Inc. Used by permission.

Illustration from *Pierre Bear* by Patsy and Richard Scarry. © 1954, Western Publishing Co., Inc. Used by permission.

Photograph (p. 62, bottom) by Kathleen Flynn from *Andy Bear: A Polar Bear Cub Grows Up at the Zoo* by Ginny Johnston and Judy Cutchins. Copyright © 1985 by Ginny Johnston and Judy Cutchins. Reprinted by permission of the publisher, Morrow Junior Books, a Division of William Morrow Co., Inc.

Illustration from *Winnie-The-Pooh* by A.A. Milne, illustrated by Ernest H. Shepard. Copyright 1926 by E.P. Dutton, renewed 1954 by A. A. Milne. Copyright under the Berne Convention. Reproduced by permission of the publisher, E.P. Dutton, a division of NAL Penguin, Inc., the Canadian publisher, Mc Clelland & Stewart, and Curtis Brown, Ltd., London.

"My Teddy Bear" by Margaret Hillert. Reprinted by permission of the author who controls all rights.

Poem and illustrations from *When We Were Very Young,* by A. A. Milne, illustrated by Ernest H. Shepard. Copyright 1924 by E.P. Dutton, renewed 1952 by A. A. Milne. Copyright under the Berne Convention. Reprinted by permission of the publisher, E. P. Dutton, a division of NAL Penguin Inc., the Canadian publisher, McClelland & Stewart, the British publisher, Methuen, and Curtis Brown, Ltd., London.

Printed in the United States of America
901 8800 987654321

Contents

From Bear to Teddy Bear

Teddy Bear is a child of the twentieth century—a much-loved child. Few toys have given rise to such a response. Before the end of his first decade, Teddy Bear had become a success all over the world. He had laid the foundations of two major toy industries and several smaller teddy bear firms, become the main character in books and comics, appeared in puzzles, paper dolls, and patterns on household goods and textiles. From the very beginning, the teddy bear was a toy for both girls and boys and a mascot for adults. This interest in and great love of teddy bears has persisted, and each year produces new teddy bear lovers despite the temptation of other new soft stuffed toys.

Many people keep their teddy bears all their lives, either on the sofa or on a shelf, or at least saved in a box in the attic. Real enthusiasts have formed teddy bear societies, arranged teddy bear picnics, and published teddy bear magazines— and even proclaimed 1985 as the Year of the Teddy Bear. A new word has been coined—arctophile, friend of the teddy bear. In 1985, the first major teddy bear auction was held at Christie's in London. But in spite of the fact that Teddy Bear has

become a collector's item, he is by no means a thing of the past. Teddy is alive and well and living all over the world!

Teddy Bear has a certain something about him, but what exactly is this

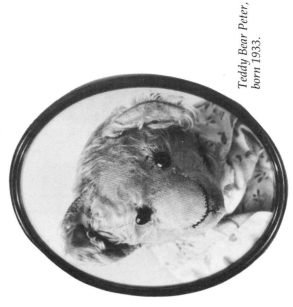

enchantment? To find the answer, it is necessary to look to the ancestor of the teddy bear—the wild bear. In northern countries, people frequently had close contact, not to say confrontations, with

7

live bears. Domestic animals were often threatened by this wild beast, this largest land predator, this terror. With its great strength and size, the bear was a worthy opponent of brave men, a prey that was respected and worshipped as divine by Lapps and other peoples.

The importance of the bear can also be found in numerous legends, hunting tales, fables, and books on its way of life

An exact copy of a teddy bear from 1904, made by the famous German toy firm of Steiff.

A bear tamer made in the 1720s in Germany for Princess Augusta Dorothea's miniature community. From Dolls and Puppets, Fritz Kredel, 1958.

and meetings between man and the King of the Forest. Tame bears were displayed at markets, where they performed tricks and walked upright. Audiences were astonished by their likeness to people and amused by their growing good nature. Long before Teddy Bear was born, both homemade wooden bears and factory-

The first Swedish exhibition of teddy bears was held in the Upplands Museum in Uppsala in 1994. Thirty thousand enthusiasts, young and old, attended. The exhibition's own teddy bear, drawn by Helny Carlsson, is shown sitting in front of the museum.

made mechanical dancing bears were created. The fact that the bear was so firmly anchored in both nature and oral tradition as an interesting and important animal perhaps made it even easier for the teddy bear to be such a success.

Today, the bear and Teddy Bear live on in many different media. They appear in books, comics, films, advertisements, and

In the new one-child Chinese family, the panda bear replaces small brothers and sisters. Poster on family planning, 1984.

political cartoons. In other words, the bear is an animal for both children and adults—an animal to which we human beings have given much import and many qualities—not two separate figures with different dispositions. The real bear is depicted as strong, but good-natured; there is no need to be afraid. The teddy bear is "spiritually" stronger, a consoler and philosopher always handy when we need him. Soft and friendly, he opens the door to our hearts.

As long ago as the seventeenth century, Scandinavians sometimes called the wild bear of the forest "Teddy Bear." From having been the name of a much-feared predator, Teddy Bear has become the name of a beloved toy. The road from beast to favorite toy is explored in this book.

9

The History of Teddy Bear

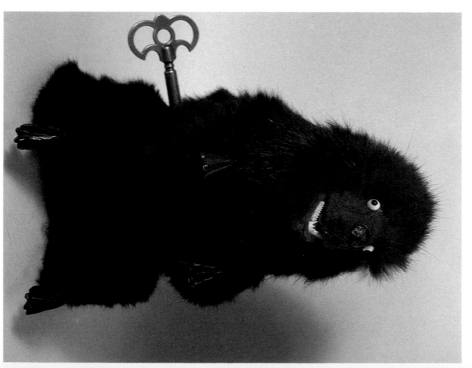

Myths about their birth and earliest childhood often arise around great personalities. Teddy Bear is no exception. The tales of his origins are numerous and they all sound like real sagas. There are two main versions, both equally exciting. One story concerns a male hero who, though not a prince, is an American president (Theodore Roosevelt). The hero goes on a bear hunt, but moved to compassion for his prey, puts down his gun. The variant is about a good-hearted woman in a wheelchair (Margarete Steiff), who with the magic of imagination and her skillful needle, conjures up a treasure-trove of toys for children. The stories run parallel but the two subjects never meet— he who is usually called the father of Teddy Bear and she who has been called his mother. Only through the teddy bear do their destinies cross.

It is still difficult to form a definitive picture of how Teddy Bear was "born," but by comparing different stories, it is possible to assemble the facts, like the pieces of a jigsaw puzzle, into one story.

Toy Animals

Not until the mid-nineteenth century did anything arise that might be called a cultural market for children, with books,

magazines, theater, and, not least, toys. Children had indeed had things to play with far back in history, and ever since the

10

Christmas card, c. 1910.

Middle Ages, craftsmen have been making toys. But industrialization first created the possibility of mass production. This capability was also the prerequisite for more people being able to afford to buy toys for their children.

A classic toy was always the farm with its house and animals made of wood. Children could also imagine they were playing with wild animals. Everything needed to build a toy zoo existed, made of tin, wood, or paper. Another common toy was Noah's Ark, with all its inhabitants grouped in families. Children could also play at circuses and let the bear dance on the floor.

Many of the wooden animals were covered with leather, but not until the 1890s did soft toys become common. The rag doll is an exception, its story older. The breakthrough for soft toys came with the Golliwog, originally the main character in a book by Florence Upton. Golly, with his black face and dishevelled hair, became an appropriate person to blame for one's own misfortunes and naughtiness.

When soft toys were introduced, a change had begun to occur in attitudes toward small children. This change arrived with the romanticism of about 1800, but now began to be widespread. Imagination and emotions were to be stimulated, and the child was to develop on its own conditions. A soft toy invited hugs and could be taken to bed. Stuffed animals could also be substitutes for living animals that country children lost when they moved into town.

When Teddy Bear made his entry, the ground was well prepared. The bear had already become a toy, and there was a whole fauna of soft animals. Teddy Bear, with his soft fur, jointed limbs, and moveable head, was a mixture of animal and doll. Small girls and boys had seen bears standing upright in zoos and at circuses, and like children, hugging each other; yet the bears of fairy tales and sagas were still wild and exciting. And as the bear has always been an object of the masculine sport of hunting, it was thus acceptable even for slightly older boys to play with a soft toy bear. By appealing to

Mechanical grizzly bear, made in France c. 1890. Stockholm Toy Museum.

11

both sexes, the teddy bear doubled his selling potential. He became the toy that could satisfy not just one but several needs.

Teddy's Bear

The name Teddy Bear is essentially English, but is also found in Germany as Teddybär. In Sweden, it still exists in the material called "teddy," though few there realize that the word came from a toy.

Behind the story of Teddy Bear stands Theodore Roosevelt, president of the United States from 1901 to 1909. The tale of Teddy Bear and the president started on a hunt in 1902. At that time, Roosevelt was taking part in negotiations over a boundary dispute between Louisiana and Mississippi. The president was an enthusiastic hunter and particularly liked hunting grizzly bears, and so, to amuse him, a bear hunt was arranged. The president was invited to fire the decisive shot, so that he would have both the honor and the hunting trophy. The bear was old and injured, as well as tied up, so Roosevelt was said to have refused either to shoot the bear or to let anyone else shoot it. That may sound rather more noble than it was: Roosevelt probably thought it unsportsmanlike to shoot a bound bear.

The story might have ended there if a cartoonist called Clifford K. Berryman hadn't come into the picture—or rather *produced* a picture. The hunting incident was reported in the *Washington Post* on November 15. The next day the newspaper returned to the topic, linking the bear with the boundary dispute. Clifford K. Berryman summarized the story in a cartoon in which the president in full hunting gear stretches out his right arm, indicating "here and no further"— marking the boundary line for both

Mississippi and the hunter. Berryman made several versions of the cartoon, and each time the bear grew smaller and smaller, to end up as a trembling little bear cub. The picture of the great hunter Roosevelt lowering his gun when faced with a defenseless creature acquired greater political importance than would simply a commentary on a boundary dispute. The cartoon went all over the world and created a lasting myth.

The next person in this American drama was a Russian immigrant in New York called Morris Michtom, who owned a little stationery and candy shop in Brooklyn. He sometimes used to enlarge his stock with toys that his wife, Rose, made. In his native country, children had played with wooden bears, and when he saw Berryman's cartoon, he thought of making a toy bear. Rose made the bear out of plush, stuffed it with wood shavings,

DRAWING THE LINE IN MISSISSIPPI.

A much-traveled, yet still well-preserved teddy bear, bought in 1904 in New York.

and gave it black shoe-button eyes. It was put in the window together with the cartoon from the paper and a little notice saying that this was "Teddy's bear." The bear immediately attracted buyers, who came in asking for more bears. Naming one bear Teddy's bear was perhaps alright, but more? So Michtom wrote to the president and asked for permission to call his bears Teddy's bears. The president agreed, although he is said to have wondered whether his name would bring much joy to the toy trade. The "historical truth" behind this exchange of letters is now part of oral tradition, for the letters are lost. Anyhow, the name was invented and the Michtoms went on making "Teddy Bears." Most teddy bears made in the United States from 1903 to 1906 were by the Michtoms. The foundations were laid for a rapidly expanding toy giant, known since 1938 as the Ideal Toy Corporation.

In the United States, there were other bearmakers, among them Adolf Gund. As early as 1898, he had a small combined store and workshop for soft toy animals in Norwalk, Connecticut. Exactly when he made his first teddy bear is uncertain, but the Gund teddy bears and other soft animals are still praised for their fine quality and design. In the 1910s, together with his partner Jacob Swedlin, Gund ran the largest soft toy industry in the United States. Swedlin later took over the whole enterprise.

In about 1906, a veritable epidemic of teddy bears broke out in the United States, and a number of new manufacturers of bears came into the field. Since not much weight was attached to brand names at that time, it is difficult to identify the teddy bears from those early days of glory.

13

A True American

Why was it that the teddy bear became such a success in the United States? One possible explanation is that it became a kind of national symbol. Bears were sold as toys as well as mascots. They became something of a "must," particularly among Americans of the lower middle class and among new immigrants.

Michtom's stroke of luck in giving the bears the president's name probably played a major part. An immigrant with one of Teddy's bears on his sofa could feel himself not only a true Republican, but also a real American. At Republican meetings and conventions, the standards were decorated with bears almost as often as with the Stars and Stripes. The bear could stand as a symbol both for the sport of bear hunting and for a test of manhood—in other words, it symbolized strength. But it also became an image of America as a young nation, where children could grow up in freedom and where their feelings were respected. As a symbol, the teddy bear was also useful on labels, clothes, textiles, and household goods. It could take up the cudgels for the president and his party in puzzles, book characters, and paper dolls. In 1906, when Theodore Roosevelt was in his second term as president, he was presented with the sixth Nobel Peace Prize for his contributions as mediator between Japan and Russia. One can almost see the peaceful American Teddy Bear leading the Russian Bear in the right direction.

The Steiff Family

The interest in the teddy bear in the United States had a great influence on its history in Europe. In the small town of Giengen, in Württemberg, Germany, in 1847, a girl named Margarete was born to the Steiff family. As a little child, she was afflicted with polio, which left her with both legs paralyzed. Despite this handicap, Margarete was able to earn her living as a dressmaker. Giengen had a large felt industry, and she made clothes and quilts out of felt. In 1880, using some leftover pieces, Margarete made a pincushion that looked like an elephant.

14

Margarete Steiff.

Children often came to see her, and they were so delighted with the elephant that she made some more and gave them away. Orders soon started pouring in, and Margarete and her brother Fritz formed a company. During the first year, the small family firm made six hundred little elephants. Then came monkeys, horses, camels, and kittens. What had once been home dressmaking became a small toy industry.

Eventually, a bear was also created (probably in 1902), which became a great success at the 1903 Leipzig Toy Fair. The idea arose from Margarete's nephew Richard, who used to draw bears at the zoo. He also suggested that the bear be

made of mohair plush, with mobile limbs and head. However, the first bears were rather coolly received, and not even the bear sent to the United States brought in orders. But on the last day of the Leipzig Fair, an American buyer caught sight of the bear. According to one story, the bear had already been packed away and had then been taken out again. The American immediately ordered three thousand bears, a huge order for those days.

Some historians maintain that Margarete Steiff was inspired by Berryman's cartoon, but this does seem unlikely. The bear was a natural development in the Steiff family's manufacturing of stuffed animals. Maybe Richard wanted to try something new, such as changing the felt to a softer material, and the plush then gave rise to the making of a bear. The great innovation was the moveable limbs, which meant the bear could stand upright as well as on all fours, just like a real bear.

Anyhow, it is true that the Steiff bears rapidly became very popular. In 1907, the

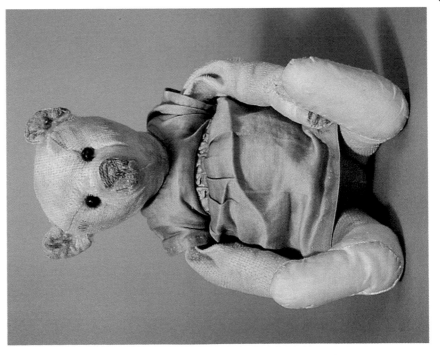

Girl teddy bear, by Steiff, c. 1905.

Top: A Steiff bear, c. 1907, mended with brown wool and given a cardigan of the same color.

Right: A Steiff bear with a clear hump, probably c. 1920s.

Bottom left: Even young elephants can play with bears. From Babar at Home, by Jean de Brunhoff, 1938.

Bottom right: Steiff bear on wheels bought it in 1917. When the ring around its neck is pulled, the bear growls.

firm made almost a million of them. When Margarete Steiff died in 1909, she left behind her a flourishing firm with a solidly established reputation for good quality and durability.

The demand for teddy bears grew and several other German firms started making them. During the First World War, the manufacture of toys declined and many firms ceased production. But Steiff survived, partly owing to their good reputation. The factory, which is still in Giengen, sells about a million teddy bears a year, most of them exported to the United States.

The Steiff teddy bear with its long nose and hump on its back is today still fairly true to nature, although its feet and hump are not quite as large as before. The Steiff bear can be recognized by the metal button in its ear—"Knopf im Ohr"—a brand label used since 1905. That was also the first year the bear acquired a "growl" in its stomach.

Other notable German manufacturers include Gebruder Hermann, founded in 1907 by Johann Hermann. In 1911, his son, Bernhard, founded his own company in Sonneburg, exporting bears to the U.S. After the Second World War, Gebruder Hermann moved to Hirschaid in West Germany. By this time Bernhard's son was running the company, which makes classic mohair bears. Current output, still produced in much the same way as in the very earliest days of the company, features a great deal of hand work.

The Grisly Company began in 1954. The name was chosen in honor of the American grizzly bear. This company makes many mohair bears, some in unusual colors such as bright red and bright green.

Schuco, a firm founded in Nuremberg in 1912, produced many very popular toys until its closing in 1970. They were the makers of the famous "yes/no" animals—two-faced Teddy Bears; they also produced miniature bears that concealed perfume bottles or compacts.

Other European Teddy Bears

In England, the Chad Valley Company existed from 1823 to 1978 when it was purchased by Palitoy, a subsidiary of the

Bears in the Butler Brothers' catalogue, 1910.

American firm General Mills, U.K. Ltd. Chad Valley began making bears and other stuffed toys in the 1920's. In 1938, they were appointed "Toymakers to Her Majesty the Queen."

Merrythought, founded in 1930 in Shropshire, is a traditional, family-owned British company. (Merrythought is the old English term for a wishbone, which is

17

The bear was well-known as a toy very early on in children's literature. From In Toy Country, by Signe Aspelin, 1911.

part of the company logo.) There is a high degree of handwork in Merrythought's bears—they still use old skills and traditional techniques, such as embroidered noses. Their director believes that their animals should be appealing near-replicas of real animals, and that a successful toy should make one smile.

Dean's Childsplay Toys has been manufacturing stuffed toys since the

early 1900's. In 1930, they were contracted by Walt Disney to make the first Mickey Mouse. The House of Nisbet has also produced a variety of Teddy Bears, including Bully Bear and the Scottish Bear. They have been making a new series of bears called "The Endangered Species"—a humorous play on words because the bears depict human types who are in danger of extinction in this modern world. The first three bears in the series are the chimney sweep, the doctor bear (who makes house calls), and the European street artist bear.

Swedish manufacture of teddy bears on a large scale did not start until after the Second World War. Today, the most well-known manufacturer is Emil Grünfeld's firm, Merimex. Grünfeld came to Sweden at the age of twenty, a refugee from the Second World War. After his elder daughter was born in 1947, he created a teddy bear for her. It was so successful that he received orders from friends and acquaintances. So it came about that Emil Grünfeld, who had thought of becoming a farmer, instead started a toy firm with his wife.

Some Teddy Bear Milestones

Today, the teddy bear appears in many guises insofar as both color and shape are concerned. Yet the original models seem to have remained. Steiff bears are still made from original patterns, and Merimex has always had to return to the traditional brown bear after every attempt to vary the model.

But there are milestones in the history of teddy bears, largely to do with color and design. The first teddy bears had the flat body of a doll. When the English started making their own bears, they changed the shape. The limbs became shorter and the bear got his round body, becoming more like a child. The German bears were filled with wood shavings, whereas the English used kapok, a soft natural material from Indonesia. The teddy bears became softer and nicer to hold.

The first teddy bears had shoe-button eyes. Later, the teddies were given glass eyes with pupils and irises, which made them look even more alive.

Emil Grünfeld with some of his teddy bears.

After the Second World War, artificial materials both outside and inside became more common. Teddy bears increasingly lost contact with their origins.

Mechanical bears from the 1960s. The polar bear lifts up the telephone receiver, while the black bear eats an egg.

19

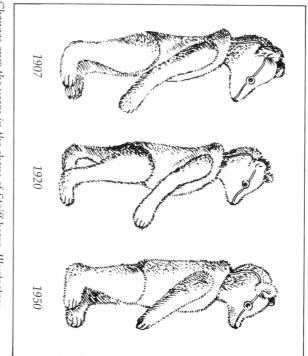

1907 1920 1950

Changes over the years in the shape of Steiff bears. Illustrator: Vera Mulder.

Not until the 1960s was there anything to compete with the teddy bear among other stuffed animal toys. During that decade, Snoopy the dog began to be manufactured, followed in the 1970s by the Pink Panther, and in the early 1980s by Garfield the cat, just to mention the most popular. Common to these three in particular is the fact that they originated from comic strips or film characters.

Collectors and Collecting

In the 1980s, interest in teddy bears has continued to grow, perhaps because the first and second generation of bear-owners, particularly in the United States and England, have continued to collect teddy bears, form Teddy Bear Societies, and even arrange Teddy Bear parties.

A 1984 survey determined that 40 percent of all bears are purchased for adults—some for investment as well as the pleasure of collecting. The Good Bears of the World is an international humanitarian association that provides teddy bears to hospitals for patients of all

When Ming, a giant panda, arrived at the London Zoo in 1930, interest in the bear-like pandas at once increased. This resulted in turn in a demand for toy pandas, which still remains. In the 1930s, the first toy koalas (a marsupial that somewhat resembles a bear) appeared in Australia. After the Second World War, they spread to Europe and the United States, where they squeezed onto the toy shelves as bears among bears.

Teddy bear belonging to Carl XVI Gustaf, king of Sweden, on a stamp, 1978.

Australian koala bear, bought 1980.

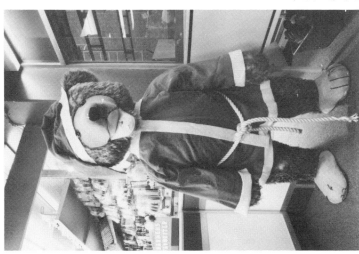

Bear, born 1965, at home on the sofa with Peter, born 1960.

ages. In their official publication, called *Bear Tracks*, they have designated October 27, Theodore Roosevelt's birthday, as Good Bear Day. The roots of this organization go back to 1951 when Russell McLean, aware that teddy bears comforted and cheered sick children, started giving bears to the hospital. His idea spread and he became known as the Teddy Bear Man. In England, Colonel Bob Henderson, in 1955, began to research teddy bears after retiring from the army. He became president of the Teddy Bear Club in 1962. The English and American groups were united as Good Bears of the World in 1970. Their first formal gathering was held in Berne, the city of the bear, in 1973.

Good Bears of the World sponsored one of the first huge bear rallies in England in 1979 at Longleat. More than 15,000 people attended. In 1981, Margaret Thatcher, England's Prime Minister, sent her bear to the second Longleat rally as did the Queen Mother, Princess Margaret, and many other notables.

In the United States, the Philadelphia Zoo's Great Bear Rally, first held in 1982, has become an annual affair with thousands of people attending. The Teddy Bear Rally in Amherst, Massachusetts, another annual event generally held the first Saturday in August, brings thousands of people to the Common in the center of town. There they can stroll around the bear exhibits, enter their own bears in competitions, and go home with special teddy bear T-shirts and other souvenirs.

Since there are more rallies and teddy bear events all the time, it's a good idea to check current Teddy Bear periodicals for listings. Teddy bear shows, which are the major source for collectible bears, are listed in these publications.

Teddy

Teddy was born in Germany in 1923. A genuine Steiff bear, he carries his years and his lineage with honor.

Teddy has lived a responsible life as companion and member of the family—first, when a young bride received him as a wedding present. Teddy was the only child the couple had, and when they were divorced in 1930, the wife gave Teddy away. She had a younger brother whose best friend had a little sister of ten called

May. May had always wanted a dog, but instead she was given Teddy to talk to. She lived in an apartment, and Teddy sat on the bed in her room. Teddy joined in the celebrations when May passed her final school exams, and eventually went on with her to college, where he sat in a corner of her dorm room and kept a firm eye on her activities. She has always been grateful to him for not writing his memoirs.

When May married, Teddy found himself with a master with a sense of humor. He was an officer in the reserve, so Teddy also had to have a uniform. When the master was called away on maneuvers, Teddy sat on the family's front porch and defended the children. Every time his master was promoted, Teddy was also promoted, but always one rank lower. Today, Teddy is an unofficial lieutenant in the reserve. For his outstanding contributions on the front porch, he has been awarded the Teddy Bear Medal and the Croix de Bear. On his sixtieth birthday, Teddy received a handsome gold medal with a picture of the president on it.

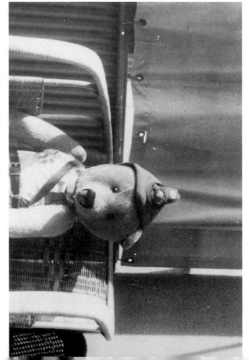

Lieutenant Teddy on the front porch.

22

Teddy thinks a great deal. Just like A. A. Milne's Winnie the Pooh, he is a bear with a very small brain, so, accordingly, are his reflections. Now and again his mistress passes along his comments, especially when a particular situation in the family can be solved best by a few words of wisdom from Teddy. This happens quite often.

Teddy has one great passion—tobogganing. It's the only sport he takes part in and he never misses a chance of watching it on television. Teddy has also been to a wedding. When May's daughter was married, he wore a top hat.

May has four grandchildren, all of whom have great respect for Teddy and play with him very carefully. Outwardly he is in very good shape (apart from his nose), which has been kissed away.

Teddy's mistress thinks that a pleasant fate.

Bear

My name's Bear and I am fifty-seven. My owner, Peter, used to kiss me every night, and often in the daytime, too. He could never go to sleep or go anywhere without me. One night I was hung up on the clothesline to dry after a bath. It was terrible for him and for me.

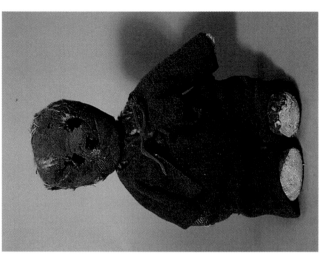

Neil

My name is Neil. I was given to a boy of three as a birthday present. When I was five, I was joined by a brother bear. Everyone thought he was very grand. They liked his white fur. And he had red leather soles! I was jealous—until they all made a fuss over me! The boy's mother made all my clothes. When I went out I wore a blue jacket and a red hood. I sometimes played cowboy, and then I wore my leather belt with pistol-holsters. My Sunday suit consists of red flannel trousers and a red shirt with N embroidered on the top pocket. My handkerchief also has N on it. My feet are rather worn, so I always have to wear a pair of white socks, which once belonged to a baby.

Twelve years ago, I retired to a cozy closet, where I live a quiet life.

Teddy Bear

A bear, however hard he tries,
Grows tubby without exercise.
Our Teddy Bear is short and fat
Which is not to be wondered at;
He gets what exercise he can
By falling off the ottoman,
But generally seems to lack
The energy to clamber back.

Now tubbiness is just one thing
Which gets a fellow wondering;
And Teddy worried lots about
The fact that he was rather stout.
He thought: "If only I were thin!
But how does anyone begin?"
He thought: "It really isn't fair
To grudge me exercise and air."

For many weeks he pressed in vain
His nose against the windowpane,
And envied those who walked about
Reducing their unwanted stout.
None of the people he could see
"Is quite" (he said) "as fat as me!"
Then, with a still more moving sigh,
"I mean" (he said) "as fat as I!"

Now Teddy, as was only right,
Slept in the ottoman at night,
And with him crowded in as well
More animals than I can tell;

Not only these, but books and things,
Such as a kind relation brings—
Old tales of "Once upon a time,"
And history retold in rhyme.

One night it happened that he took
A peep at an old picture-book,
Wherein he came across by chance
The picture of a King of France
(A stoutish man) and, down below,
These words: "King Louis So and So,
Nicknamed 'The Handsome!'" There he sat,
And (think of it!) the man was fat!

Our bear rejoiced like anything
To read about this famous King,
Nicknamed "The Handsome." There he sat,
And certainly the man was fat,
Nicknamed "The Handsome." Not a doubt
The man was definitely stout.
Why then, a bear (for all his tub)
Might yet be named "The Handsome Cub!"

"Might yet be named." Or did he mean
That years ago he "might have been"?
For now he felt a slight misgiving:
"Is Louis So and So still living?

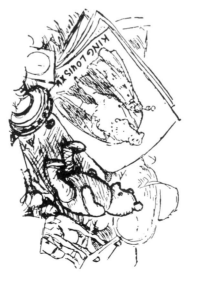

24

Fashions in beauty have a way
Of altering from day to day.
Is 'Handsome Louis' with us yet?
Unfortunately I forget."

Next morning (nose to windowpane)
The doubt occurred to him again.
One question hammered in his head:
"Is he alive or is he dead?"
Thus, nose to pane, he pondered; but
The lattice window, loosely shut,
Swung open. With one startled "Oh!"
Our Teddy disappeared below.

There happened to be passing by
A plump man with a twinkling eye,
Who, seeing Teddy in the street,
Raised him politely to his feet,
And murmured kindly in his ear
Soft words of comfort and of cheer:
"Well, well!" "Allow me!" "Not at all."
"Tut-tut! A very nasty fall."

Our Teddy answered not a word;
It's doubtful if he even heard.
Our bear could only look and look:
The stout man in the picture-book!
That "handsome" King—could this be he,
This man of adiposity?
"Impossible," he thought. "But still,
No harm in asking. Yes I will!"

"Are you," he said, "by any chance
His Majesty the King of France?"
The other answered, "I am that,"
Bowed stiffly, and removed his hat;
Then said, "Excuse me," with an air,
"But is it Mr. Edward Bear?"
And Teddy, bending very low,
Replied politely, "Even so!"

They stood beneath the window there,
The King and Mr. Edward Bear,
And, handsome, if a trifle fat,
Talked carelessly of this and that . . .
Then said His Majesty, "Well, well,
I must get on," and rang the bell.
"Your bear, I think," he smiled. "Good-day!"
And turned, and went upon his way.

A bear, however hard he tries,
Grows tubby without exercise
Our Teddy Bear is short and fat,
Which is not to be wondered at.
But do you think it worries him
To know that he is far from slim?
No, just the other way about—
He's *proud* of being short and stout.

From *When We Were Young* by A.A. Milne, 1945. Illustrated by Ernest H. Shepard

Little Bear in the Red Cottage

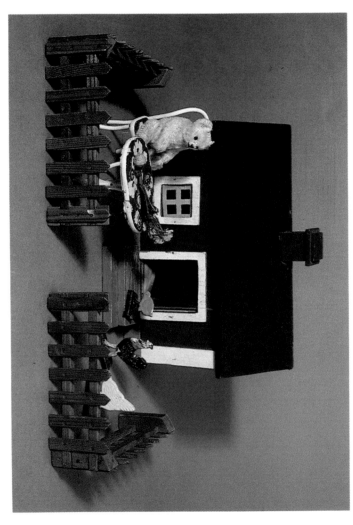

I am a little bear and I live in a red house. The house was originally built about 1930 and was a Christmas present to a small girl called Ella. I moved in a few Christmas Eves later. Inside the fenced-in yard lived a rooster, a hen, and their little chickens—and rabbits, the of course. The house stood on a red silk handkerchief on Ella's chest-of-drawers. When I was first introduced to Ella, I sat by the bell on the handle of her first bicycle.

The furniture in the house is fairly simple, a table and two chairs, but quite sufficient for my needs. I used to have visits from other little bears who lived

with Ella's brother and sister. In those days, I often wore crocheted pants and a sweater, and had a little cap on one ear. When we went to a party, we all had silk dresses with ruffles, and at night we slept in embroidered flannel shirts. Aunt Martha made all our clothes.

We also mixed quite a lot with dolls and other animals. Sometimes we went to the Big House, where Grandmother had a dollhouse with a kitchen, bedrooms, and two living rooms. The thirties were a good time. These days, I am mostly alone and sit going over my old memories. That's not bad, either.

26

· Bear News ·

Mischka

Mischka is a handsome, wise old bear. He was given to a little Russian girl in St. Petersburg in 1908, and the two have been inseparable ever since. Her beloved stepfather gave him to her. The girl's name was Zoya, and she eventually became an artist in Sweden. But in 1908, neither she nor Mischka knew anything about their future. They lived in the warm sheltered world of games in the big nursery and outings to the park, and spent their summers at the beaches in the Crimea or in the Caucasus mountains. World War I and then the Revolution changed everything. Zoya's stepfather was killed, and with Mother and Grandmother, Mischka and Zoya moved to Moscow, where Zoya studied and worked. After a brief spell in prison, Zoya was rescued, then taken to Sweden when

Zoya with cousins on a park bench in St. Petersburg, c. 1910.

she married Karl Kilhom. Mischka went with Zoya to this new country journeying in a hat-box, packed in together with some icons. That was all the luggage Zoya had, and at first the Russian customs official regarded Mischka with great suspicion. But in the end they both got permission to leave the country.

In Sweden, Zoya went on with her training as an artist, and Mischka became a faithful friend in her studio. Nowadays he sits there all day on an old embroidered cushion from Russia and keeps a watchful eye on Zoya when she is painting. Mischka listens to all the conversations between Zoya and her models, but he is very discreet and knows how to keep a secret.

Aches and Pains

Like all people and animals, Teddy Bear has his ailments and illnesses. Many bear owners and writers have described the hardships their teddy bears have undergone. However, it is unclear whether the bear goes to the doctor or to the veterinarian to find cures for his ill health.

Ask your master to knit you a pair of good soles. They're very nice to have in the winter.

Teddy Bear, born 1933

I have also been given new feet, but unfortunately they're a little drafty. They were sewn on very carelessly. I have become both ragged and worn out in my old age, anyhow. Wouldn't it be great if I got a new coat!

Teddy Bear Anderson, born about 1915

Ugh, I'm so miserable! My feet are worn out and my wood shavings are coming out. What shall I do?

Teddy Bear Libby, born 1919

I've been given a new fur coat several times. I was just as bald as you are, but now I've been quite restored.
Pellerinchen, born 1921

I went to the dolls' party and ate too much ice cream. How my stomach aches. Ay, ay!
Teddy Pearson, born 1930

This huge bandage is exactly what I need in this sad situation.
Teddy Frank, born 1960

My striped cotton heart is good, too. Bandages get dirty so quickly. Just look at my bandaged arm!
Bruno Bear, born 1930s

I have had several operations. I was given a new button eye, a new red nose, and yellow patches on my ears. There was nothing really wrong with me, but my owner thought I looked more handsome like this.
Buddy Bear, born 1947

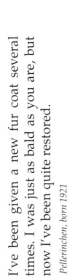

The Doll Doctor

In Margaret Wise Brown's *The Doll Doctor*, the kindly old man who visits the injured teddy is clearly an M.D.—as we can see by the initials on his bag. The good old doctor, who *still* makes house calls, comes running when Teddy Bear falls and hurts himself. Clearly, the little patient, who has been put to bed with a compress on his head, now feels much, much better.

From *Dr. Squash and the Doll Doctor* by Margaret Wise Brown, 1955

30

My Teddy Bear

A teddy bear is nice to hold.
The one I have is getting old.
His paws are almost wearing out
And so's his funny, furry snout
From rubbing on my nose of skin,
And all his fur is pretty thin.
A ribbon and a piece of string
Makes a sort of necktie thing.
His eyes came out and now instead
He has some new ones made of thread.
I take him everywhere I go
And tell him all the things I know.
I like the way he feels at night,
All snuggled up against me tight.

by Margaret Hillert

Illustrations by Jean Claverie. From The Bear and Henry, by Arlene Blanchard, 1987.

31

A Place Where You Faint

Before the three dolls, Elsie, Tina, and Lizzy, and the bears, Ivan and Steven, could go to Sweden as child refugees from Finland, they had to have health certificates. Clever Elsie knows where they can get them and she firmly whisks her companions to the health center.

They came to a place called Help! and Elsie knew the people there were able to say whether you were sick or healthy, and they had to have a certificate to say so if they were to be allowed to go.

A little lady in nurse's uniform and with a bun at the back of her neck was sitting at a table, and she had seen so many peculiar patients, she wasn't at all surprised to see these five. All they had to do was to stand in line and then she took out some strange tubes and things.

"Death and torment!" said Teddy Bear Ivan, quickly getting behind Elsie.

"Now just be brave," the nurse said. I'm only going to prick your arm, just a little prick. It doesn't hurt at all. Tuberculosis test," she said to another lady in a white apron, and who gave her a little glass stick with which she placed a few drops of liquid on Elsie's arm. Then she took what appeared to be a sharp little pen and prick!—little red roses spread out in the drops.

Elsie stood up straight and brave, because she was in a hurry. "And now, where are the bears?"

"Clever girls," said the nurse quickly, because she was in a hurry. "And now, where are the bears?"

Well now, that was another matter. Elsie looked all around.

Teddy Ivan had crawled behind her knees, making himself as small as possible. And where was Teddy Steven?

He was stretched out flat on the floor. He'd fainted.

"Now, now," said the nurse sternly. She splashed water onto Teddy Steven's pale little nose, which was sticking straight up in the air. "Oh, you bears. You've got such hairy skin," she went on, "you won't feel a thing!"

"Teddy Ivan, if you're good, you can play cards on the floor of the plane," whispered Elsie, because she was ashamed. She pulled him up, although he made himself as heavy as a sack of sand. But the lady took Teddy Steven on her knees and pricked him almost before he came to. Teddy Ivan was ashamed afterwards, too, because it was nothing. For a brave bear like him.

But what about Tina?

They'd forgotten all about her. Elsie looked for her all over the place and then the lady got up to look, too, and almost fell over. Yes, there Tina was, sitting under the nurse's skirts as quiet as a mouse. Tina tried to pull away, but no matter how hard she kicked, the nurse held onto her other arm.

"Oh, goodness," said Elsie, almost in tears by the time it was over and they all had white bandages on their arms. "What a nuisance you're all being. I don't want to go with you at all!"

But the lady had to do diphtheria tests too, and put a stick down their throats, and look up their noses. You never heard such spitting and coughing and hiccoughing. The nurse could hardly hear

herself speak. "Calm down, children, calm down," she said. "Now, please calm down."

When she tickled Teddy Ivan's nose, he sneezed so violently that the neat little white cap on her head flew right off. "Oh, help!" shouted Teddy Ivan. But Teddy Steven picked up the cap and gave it back with a polite bow, because he was quite wide awake now.

"Now, now," said the nurse again. Then she called out: "Doctor! Doctor!"

A tall man in a white coat was just going past the door.

"Doctor, dear, would you write out a certificate for these children?" Then she was relieved to have some other patients to deal with.

The doctor picked up all the dolls and bears and put them on a table, then examined them carefully. They sat in a straight row in front of him, and he squeezed their stomachs and looked down their throats. When he squeezed the

bears, it went "aaaaahhhh" inside them, as if they were sighing heavily. Once upon a time they had been able to growl really well, but the machinery had gone rusty. The doctor had a nice snub nose and looked young. Perhaps he had children of his own, because he said, "I could do with some bears like this." Then he pinched their ears.

"Doctor," whispered Elsie, plucking up courage. "Doctor, please write that we're healthy, otherwise we won't be able to go today. Then we won't find our mothers. They've already gone by boat. And we are healthy. Please, please, doctor!"

"Hm," said the doctor. He scratched in Teddy Ivan's fur to see if he had any fleas, because there were lots of questions about that on the certificate.

"Hm. Do you itch?" he said.

"What?"

"Do you itch?"

"What?"

"Do you itch, I said?"

"I-t-c-h, four letters. Perhaps that'll go," said Teddy Ivan. He was staring at the doctor's checked necktie and thinking what a good crossword that would make.

"No, I dddddd ..." And he bent double, because the doctor had poked him in the stomach.

"That'll teach you," said the doctor, looking just like a little boy. "Have you made your way here all by yourselves?"

"Yes, indeed... death and torment," said Teddy Ivan, straightening up in his green jacket.

"Then I suppose you must go on," said the doctor, and he cut out five small pieces of paper and wrote on them that tests had been made and they were healthy and had no fleas.

From Teddy Bear's Journey by Solveig von Schoultz, 1944. Illustrated by Tove Jansson.

Doctor Brown

I went to my mistress over seventy years ago. When she and her sisters were ill, I kept them company. That's why I'm called Doctor Brown. One of the girls made me a Tyrolean costume and I've also got some flowered clogs.

One year I was in hibernation. The girls had forgotten me out in a hedge. It was very cold and unpleasant. I thought afterwards I would never again go out-of-doors in the winter.

I live a quiet life now, as a mascot. I've gotten rather worn over the years, but they've patched me up with tape, almost as good as in a real hospital.

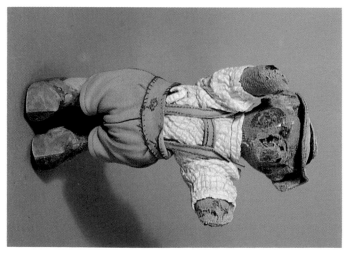

Eugene and Eugenia

My name is Eugene and I used to work at the hospital, where I comforted young patients. I made many friends there. One even embroidered a thank-you on the soles of my feet.

My girlfriend's name is Eugenia. The nurses made her out of real lambskin. Some people think she's rather silly, but I like her. We're both retired on a pension now, and we live in a cottage by the ocean.

This is what it says on my feet: "Dear Eugene. Thank you for the night of July 1, 1943, when you calmed my heart."

A Safe Teddy Bear with Firmly Attached Eyes

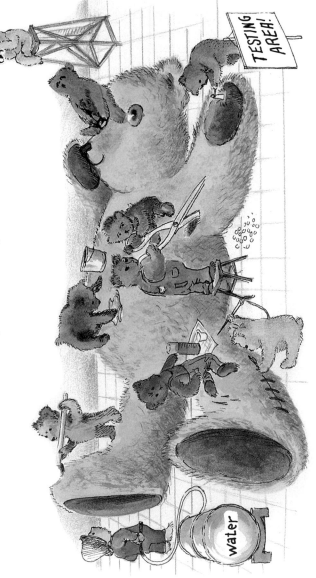

A teddy bear has to fulfill certain safety regulations. In addition, there are a number of recommendations made by the Consumer Product Safety Commission and other consumer groups.

  * A teddy bear's eyes and nose must not come off easily. Try pulling them! Eyes should be acrylic—not glass; they should be attached with safety-lock fasteners—not pins.

  * A teddy bear for small children should not have loose ribbons, bells, or any other parts that could be detached and swallowed.

  * A teddy bear should be washable.

  * A teddy bear keeps its shape better and its stuffing in place if it has double covering.

  * A teddy bear should have no sharp parts.

  * *Good* stuffing: polyester, wool, cotton waste, kapok, or body of whole foam plastic.

  * *Bad* stuffing: plastic beads, crushed nutshells, marbles, shredded plastic foam. Small children can easily be suffocated if they get any of these materials down their throats.

  * There are few *fireproof* bears. The exceptions are bears made of modacrylic fiber, which is more expensive than other materials.

Robert was naughty.

Mona's most beloved bear, Teddy Bear Muffin, was lying on the unpainted nursery table in a ray of sunlight coming from the window, his stomach still wet and sewn up with black wool after Robert's operation. His black button eyes shone in the sun, but he looked exhausted and thin.

How could Robert be so nasty, Robert, whom she loved and admired?

It had begun after breakfast.

While they were sitting at the table, Robert said to Mom that he was going to be a doctor when he was big. Mom laughed and said we would see. Mona said nothing, but she bit into her toast and thought to herself that Robert was already big, because he went to school.

Yes, that's what Robert was going to be. He had decided that the day before when the doctor had listened to his heart through a long tube.

Mona was sitting quietly thinking. She didn't at all like that fat doctor who tickled her chest when he put his head down on it, or rubbed ointment into her arms so it stung, and gave her medicine that tasted nasty because she was always wetting herself. A doctor—that was someone who hurt you…

Robert flung away his napkin and got down from the table. At that moment, he caught sight of the shabby old Muffin on the chair beside Mona.

"Muffin's ill," he said. "I'll listen to him."

"He's not ill," said Mona crossly. But Robert snatched Muffin and ran into the nursery. Mona slid off her chair

and rushed after him with her half-eaten toast in her hand. But Mom grabbed her so that she couldn't get away.

"Wait now—wipe your mouth and ask to get down."

"Forwhatwehavejustreceivedmay thelordmakeustrulythankful," she said, curtseying to God, kissing Mama's hand and then rushing out.

When Mona got into the nursery, Robert was leaning over Muffin with a pen on his chest as if he were listening in. He was frowning, with an important expression on his face.

"Yes, yes—he's very sick," he said solemnly. "We must operate."

"No!" shrieked Mona. "He's not sick, he's not at all sick!"

Robert looked at her in a superior way.

"You wouldn't understand," he said.

"I do because I'm a doctor. It's appendicitis. He'll get better, you'll see."

"No, I don't want it, I don't want it," cried Mona, stamping her foot.

Robert smiled.

"Don't be silly now—look, you've gone and wet yourself again. Mama…"

Mona was miserable. It came by itself. She couldn't help it, and she started to scream, because she couldn't help it, because Robert was going to operate on Muffin, because she could do nothing about it.…

"Poor little thing," said Mama and took her into the bedroom. "And you've got no dry panties. You can have a pair of mine."

Mom tried to console her, but Mona didn't want to be consoled. She quickly wriggled out of her mother's arms and rushed into the nursery, the lace flapping

"Now you'll see—how fine he'll be," Robert went on. With quick, hard fingers, he tore a handkerchief into strips and stuffed them into the hole. "I'll just sew up the wound now," said Robert. Mom had taught him how to sew and he frowned heavily as he threaded the needle and sewed with large crooked stitches.

"Why is there such a big wound?" said Mona. "It's terribly ugly."

"Stupid," snapped Robert. "I had to be able to get at it. What are you crying about? Then we have to wash the wound, too." He dipped the handkerchief into the cup and splashed water on liberally, several times. Water went all over the table and Muffin was soaked through.

"Robert," called Mom. "Come on now. Time for your story. Hurry up."

"Yes, I'm coming . . . Wait a minute . . . we'll operate on the other bears later on. Maybe we'll have to take off Paul's arm. Look how ragged he is there."

But Mona snatched Paul to her. "He's not," she said.

"Stupid . . ." Robert began.

"Well, are you coming, Robert?"

"Yes, yes," said Robert and ran out.

The door banged behind him and Mona stayed behind with Paul in her arms. She wiped Muffin's stomach with the remains of the handkerchief and put him in the sun to dry. He smelled so peculiar when he was wet.

Perhaps it was great to be operated on, to be cut open and then sewn up again—there was something special about it. But she thought Muffin looked really rather miserable, miserable and ugly. Ugly—but anyway, he was her own Muffin and she didn't love him any the less for that.

Eva Alexanderson, *Me When Little*, 1955.
Illustrator, Vera Mulder.

round her legs. Robert was standing there, looking as important as before, and he had just cut a hole in Muffin's stomach. He had a cup of water beside him, together with a ball of wool.

"No—I don't want it, I don't want it," mumbled Mona, more faintly this time. To think that Robert dared, to think that he could do such a thing! Muffin didn't resist at all, but just lay there letting Robert cut right in the middle of his stomach with the scissors. Reluctantly admiring, Mona stood watching her brother, her sobs stuck in her throat. No one could stop Robert from doing what he wanted to do.

"See this," said Robert, poking some wood shavings out of the bear's stomach. "Here's his appendix. It's out now."

"Is it?" whispered Mona. "Is that his appendix?"

"Of course—we'd better take out a little more... like that, then it'll all be clean."

He took out some more of the crackling entrails and Muffin grew quite thin. Mona couldn't say a thing.

In the early 1970s, D.K. Blackmore, D.G. Young, and C.M. Young, English veterinary surgeons, carried out the first scientific investigation of Teddy bears. Here is a short extract from their work.

A total of 1,598 examples of *Brunus Edwardii* were examined. Of the 1,600 owners quoted, 1,599 agreed to have their bears examined and the majority could even provide a comprehensive case history of the bear. One example was excluded because it was placed in quarantine when its owner contracted German measles.

Attempts to register body temperature were abandoned because all of the examples appeared to have a constant temperature. Each bear underwent a thorough external examination, and information on age, weight, state and color of coat, and any physical handicaps were noted. The condition of the filling was examined with thorough palpation. Where necessary, X-rays were taken. Deeper internal tissue often protruded from surface injuries and, in some cases, a small incision was made in a seam, samples extracted, and the injuries sewn up again with bear cotton thread and a darning needle.

The psychological state of the bear was judged either by analytical procedures or by scrutinizing health records with special regard to the frequency and extent of contact with children.

Results of Survey

A total of 1,598 animals and diverse appendages were examined. Attempts were made to classify the results, but as the causality in nearly all the cases was due to

more than one factor, it was not possible to decide the true primary cause. Similar injuries appeared on many different parts of the body, which meant that no separate description was possible. No disease organisms could be isolated, and the dominant cause of a majority of morbid changes was external violence.

Some cases are described here in greater depth to exemplify the complex causal connection and consequent manifestations of sickness in this species.

Case 1. A six-month-old bear owned by a four-year-old boy was found to be suffering from acute neck sprain as well as the loss of one leg. The animal's general state of health was good and its coat was of normal thickness. The injury was due to the results of a dispute over its ownership. Treatment of the neck was manual counter-twisting of the head (which had been turned sideways), and surgical reattachment of the leg was free of complications.

Case 3. A ten-year-old bear had been owned by three siblings in turn. Its normally yellow coat was changed. It was dirty gray, and showed considerable hair loss, and only in certain places on the nose, ears, and extremities was the original bear cotton thread still evident. Arm holes and groin seams were weakened causing the extremities to be displaced, but no rupture of the filling was observed. Repeated transportation by only one limb was the main cause of the chronic weakness, for which there was no satisfactory treatment.

Bears of the World

Teddy Bear has ancient and magnificent origins—his ancestors the wild bears. His most important ancestor is the brown bear. Next come the polar bear and the black bear. Not all species of bear have had the honor of becoming a toy, and some teddy bears stem not from bears but from bearlike animals, such as the koala and the giant panda.

Ties with ancestors were previously much stronger. In the childhood of Teddy Bear, children knew they were playing with a bear. Today they play with a teddy. However, it is important not to forget the real bears and other prototypes.

The Brown Bear

Brown bears are found in Europe, Asia, and North America. They live mostly in forest regions. A hundred years ago, they were threatened with extinction, but now, slowly but surely, they seem to be on the increase.

Brown bears.
School poster
by Friedrich Specht,
c. 1890.

39

Grizzly. Ahus glass. Designed by Arno Schmuck.

The brown bear is very fond of berries, but also likes to feast on ants, various plants, and honey. It digs up roots with its long claws and grubs about in anthills. The bear also eats flesh, both of animals and any carrion it finds. As a scavenger, it helps keep the forest clean.

The bears generally live alone except during the mating season. Young cubs stay with the mother for the first few years. In late autumn, when berries and plants begin to be less plentiful, the bear goes into a deep sleep similar to hibernation, except that its body temperature is not reduced and its bodily functions continue. It then sleeps until spring. During this long winter sleep, the bear lives off the fat it has stored during intensive feeding, up to twenty hours a day, in the summer and autumn. The female does not sleep all the time, but gives birth during hibernation. She usually has two cubs every other year. When the cubs are born, they are blind and helpless, scarcely bigger than rats.

There are several species of brown bears. The *grizzly bear*, also called silvertip, once roamed all over North America, but it has now been driven away by man and is found mostly in the western part of North America, especially Alaska and Canada. The grizzly is known as a skillful salmon fisher, but also has the reputation of being particularly dangerous and aggressive toward people. Many adventure stories relate how both Indians and settlers fought this bear. In actual fact, the grizzly attacks only if it is threatened. Like most bears, it lives the life of a recluse and avoids approaching us two-legged creatures. Grizzlies weigh from 300 to 1,600 pounds.

The *kodiak bear*, which lives in Alaska, is the largest living land predator in the world. None of the bears living today, however, are as large as the giant cave bears of the Ice Age.

From Burre-Busse's Journey to the North Pole, by Cyrus Grané, 1921. Illustrated by Louis Moe.

Profile of brown bear.

Profile of polar bear.

The Sloth Bear

A large bear that does not often appear as a toy is the *sloth bear*. On the other hand, it is forever linked with Baloo in Kipling's *Jungle Book*. It lives in the jungles of India and Sri Lanka, where it still performs as a dancing bear. The sloth bear is very fond of fruit, sugar cane, honey, flowers, and eggs, but insects most of all. Its long mobile snout and very long narrow tongue enable it to suck up termites and other insects.

The Polar Bear

Next to the Kodiak bear, the *polar bear* is the largest land predator. It ranges in length from seven to almost nine feet. The largest ever weighed was heavier than a small car.

Polar bears live in the Arctic and eat mainly flesh and fish, because there is not much else to choose from. Top of the menu are seals, which they catch by lying in wait at the breathing holes in the ice. The polar bear has sharper claws and teeth than other bears, so has adapted to the prey available in the arctic regions.

In Hudson Bay in Canada, however, there are polar bears that live in the forest, and some of them have discovered that they can find food on garbage heaps. No one is pleased to see such visitors, and attempts have been made to stun them with drugged darts and take them away

From Animal Life, by Alfred Brehmn, 1874, illustrated by Robert Kretschmer.

from towns. But the garbage-loving bears obstinately lumber back to the places where they have learned there is plenty of food.

Not all polar bears sleep through the winter, for they can hunt seal just as well then. The females that are to give birth, however, dig themselves down into snowdrifts to be slightly warmer for a few months.

The American Black Bear

The *American black bear*, *Ursus Americanus*, is mostly vegetarian. It lives in forests and is a good climber. This bear averages five feet in length and weighs 200 to 500 pounds. Black bears are shy and generally unaggressive except in some of the National Parks where they have lost their fear of man and have become

nighttime raiders of campgrounds and garbage dumps.

Actually "black bears" are not always black. They can be cinnamon, white, or even blue. Kermode's bear is small and almost pure white. It lives on Gribble Island and environs in British Columbia. The blue, or glacier, bear is a rare color phase of the American black bear living mostly on the Yakutat Peninsula in Alaska. Most of the Yakutat bears are black but carry the genes which can cause the coat to turn a beautiful gun-metal blue. Unfortunately the color makes the pelts very desirable to hunters and the

43

m The Black and ite Bear, by Hiroyuki ...ahashi, 1976.

From *Animal Life*, by Brehm, 1882. Illustrated by Gustav Mützel.

bears are in danger of disappearing. In 1972, the U.S. Coast Guard and personnel from the San Diego Zoo cooperated in the rescue of a young blue bear who was then transported to the San Diego Zoo where he became part of an effort to breed more blue bears.

Bearlike Animals— the Giant Panda and the Koala

The *giant panda,* which really does look like a huge black-and-white living teddy bear, is very rare. The first European to describe this timid animal was a French missionary, Father David, in 1869.

The giant panda is to be found only in a limited area in Szechuan in China, where it lives mostly on bamboo shoots. Only about 1,000 pandas are left in the world. If the pandas' food should succumb to drought or clearing, they cannot survive. The Chinese have worked for years to prevent their extinction. Many pandas have twins, but they usually bring up only one of them. Most attempts to feed abandoned cubs have hitherto been unsuccessful.

Some zoologists consider the pandas to be semi-bears, while others think they are either a member of the raccoon family or an animal species of their own.

The *koala* is not a bear, either, although it has been the model for a number of toy bears. It is the size of a large teddy bear and can weigh up to thirty-five pounds. Its fur was once used to make toy koalas, a practice now prohibited.

The koala is a marsupial (like the kangaroo) and has a pocket in its abdomen in which the young koala lives for six months. The koala lives in Australia and keeps to the eucalyptus trees, eating the leaves. Any threat to the eucalyptus is also a threat to the koalas.

This pleasant little koala is in the series *Boner's Ark* by Mort Walker and Frank Johnson.

Advertisement for Finesse Face Cloths, 1985.

The Racoon

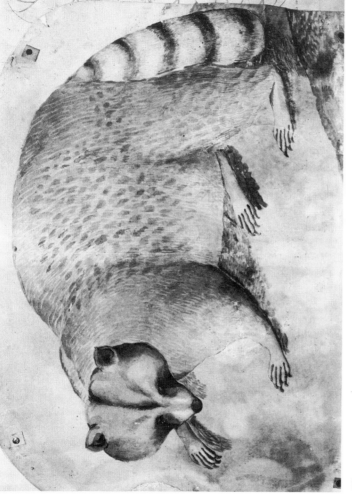

The raccoon Siupp from Carl von Linnaeus' Hammerby. "His temperament," writes Linnaeus, "was to be stubborn, and that to a great extent, so that when he was led on a rope, he would in no way tolerate one pulling on the rope, but then at once lie down on the ground, arms and feet splayed out, refusing to go with stick, but with friendly means, and when one wished to catch him, he defended himself with teeth and claws, mumbling like a bear."

An animal that often appears in advertisements and stories is the *raccoon*, which is also popular as a toy. The raccoon, or coon, is generally believed to be a relative of the panda. Sometimes called a "wash bear," by Europeans, it is frequently observed washing its food before eating. In fact, this is an instinctive movement that wild raccoons make in water when they are catching crayfish, for instance, one of their favorite foods. Otherwise the raccoon mostly eats what it can find: berries, fruit, acorns, oats, insects, eggs, and small rodents, as well as fish.

The racoon is found mostly in America, from Mexico up to Canada. Smaller groups were introduced into Europe in the 1930s. They like living in deciduous forests, where they make their nests in hollow trees.

Bears generally live alone, but raccoons live in family groups. Many American raccoons live near human beings—or, more specifically, near garbage cans. Since raccoons can spread diseases, they are frequently hunted as pests. Their long, thick fur has been used to make coats, as well as the coonskin hats of frontier days, which bore the striped tail as ornament.

45

From a Bear's Diary

November 3rd

Started snowing. Not warm. I'm cold. Thought I'd hibernate. Found no good spot all morning. Where are all the places? Dug in the earth under the snow. Got nothing but exercise.

Decided to find my old den. Actually got there in the afternoon. Messy. But went to bed. Wasn't sleepy. Couldn't go to sleep. Went out. Still snowing. Went for a walk in the snow. Had nothing to do.

Winter housing for bears. Illustrator: Vera Mulder.

November 10th

Can't find my way back to my old den. Have to try to find another. Haven't seen anything—or anyone. Still snowing and not warm. I make big tracks. Must have grown since last year. How odd.

Went past Olaf. He was hibernating in a—tree. Sleeping with his paws hanging down. Oh, well. Yes, yes. Thought of waking him, but yes, yes. Started to get tired. I last ate five days ago. How odd.

From The Bear That Wanted to Be a Bear, by Frank Tashlin, 1959.

November 13th

Gone past three inhabited hibernation places during the last few hours. Things lying asleep in them. Without any tracks.

I loped along, yawning so that the snow went right down into my stomach. Always something. Thought a lot about Olaf and climbed up a tree. Struck me as not so bad. Made a large hole when I fell. I didn't see any hole under Olaf's tree. I don't like Olaf—any longer.

Found my old place, by the way. Nice and tidy. Draft-proofed and warm. And full. Very full—and warm.

46

February 15th

Must have fallen asleep. Tried to turn over. Couldn't.

April 16th

Woke up properly. The side I'd been lying on all winter is still asleep. Thin and wretched as usual. Went out and stretched. You do get sort of stiff—depends on what the place is like, of course.

It was spring. Scratched in the ground. Broke a claw.

But it's s p r i n g.

From *Animals who do not ...* Beppe Wolger, 1956.

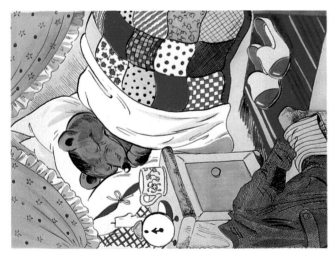

From Animals of the Forest, *by Lucie Lundberg, 1954.*

November 16th

Autumn no longer here. What a lot you meet then! Not a day without occupied places. What pleasant talks—what friendliness, what hospitality, what—what a winter!

The bear's asleep, the bear's asleep in his peaceful cave.
He's harmless
as long as you're careful,
but all the same,
but all the same
you can never quite—TRUST HIM!

November 20th

Might actually *become* a place to spend the winter. With a little labor. And patience. And—ingenuity. That Olaf—he.... No, can't be bothered to think about him. I've packed it all round with—*snow*, with *snow*, when other bears use... but it'll have to do. I tried it out in the morning. Rather cramped, perhaps, and scratchy, and not all that warm yet—autumn *has* gone. But perhaps it'll be alright, though the location, the location ...

47

Bear Hunt

Bear Hunting in Europe

There were plenty of bears in the European forests in the old days. They traveled around, helping themselves to food in cattle pastures and sheep pens. Of course, people wanted to protect their domestic animals and, as far back as the Middle Ages, they organized hunts for bears, wolves, and lynx. The hunts often lasted for several days, and both men and women took part in them, armed with axes, spears, and cudgels. Hunting was best in winter, when animal tracks were

Bear Hunt in Dalarna, Sweden, 1827. Fifteen hundred people took part in the hunt, which lasted for six days. From Fieldsports of the North, by Llewellyn Lloyd, 1830.

48

The triumphant return. After a bear hunt in Dalsland, Sweden, in 1836, the dead bear is carried on poles by four strong men, the procession headed by some musicians included to cheer up the hunters, but also to frighten the bears. The man in the checked trousers is probably Lloyd himself. From Adventures in Scandinavia, by Llewellyn Lloyd, 1854. detail.

easy to follow. The prey was surrounded by a chain of hundreds of people there to see that no predator got away.

Some of the last great bear hunts took place in Sweden during the first half of the nineteenth century. By then the number of bears had been enormously reduced, and a great many people were pleased the hated "cattle raiders" would soon be exterminated. Others thought it a pity if a few bears were not allowed to remain, at least in national parks. In 1893, the Swedish Parliament decided that the state could no longer pay a bounty on bears, and from then on bears were protected in Sweden. In the Soviet Union, which is also rich in forests, bear hunts have been common until today.

Bear Hunting in North America

The black bear was hunted by the Indians for food and fur. It was venerated by many of the tribes and, because it could walk

A scene from Theodore Roosevelt's hunting adventures is recreated in a 1953 advertisement for Steiff bears.

erect like a man, Indians felt a kinship for it even while they hunted it. They would hold ceremonies of apology before the hunt and observed ritual treatment of the carcass afterwards. Until the arrival of the European settlers, the black bears thrived in the East; but the farmers and builders, regarding them as "varmints," gradually killed or drove them off. Farmers hunted them out of necessity and sportsmen because they found them to be the only dangerous American big game. Bears were pursued by individual hunters and by hunting parties, some of which used packs of dogs. They were also trapped.

49

King Carl XII of Sweden tries to kill a bear with nothing but a club. It is fortunate that the man with the pitchfork is hurrying to his aid. From King Carl XII and his Warriors, by Petter Westlin, 1859. Illustrated by G. Wahlbom.

The bears in Florida survived because swamp terrain made for difficult hunting conditions. In the Northeast, the deeply forested mountainous areas became the bear's last refuge.

The grizzly was once plentiful on the West coast, ranging all the way from Mexico to Alaska. Due to its fierce nature and great strength it was not often hunted by Indians. When white men first encountered it, they discovered that their light Kentucky rifles were of little use

Below: Between life and death. From Adventures in Scandinavia, by Llewellyn Lloyd, 1854.

Just like a human, Teddy Nilsson fishes for salmon and hunts moose. From Pierre Bear *by Patsy and Richard Scarry, 1954.*

and as part of their legends. The early Eskimos used spears and arrows in the hunt, sometimes tricking the bear into coming close enough to attack by disguising themselves as seals. Now the bear is hunted with guns. It has become prized as a trophy by sports hunters and, until rather recently, was even hunted by aircraft. The polar bear is now considered to be an endangered species and is protected by an agreement among Canada, Denmark, Norway, the Soviet Union, and the United States. The native peoples of the northern regions are allowed to kill polar bears for their own use and only by traditional methods. Since polar bears are so widely dispersed, a population of fifteen to twenty thousand is deemed necessary to maintain the species. It is hoped that these restrictions will save the polar bear.

against an enraged grizzly bear. The settlers were not able to coexist with the grizzly; therefore, with the transition to heavier caliber rifles, the grizzly was successfully hunted and nearly exterminated in the lower forty-eight states. Today, a comparative few grizzlies remain in the National Parks. They are more numerous in Alaska and Canada where they are not forced into conflict with man.

The polar bear has always been important to the Eskimos as a test of a hunter's strength, as a symbol of power,

51

More Tame Than Wild

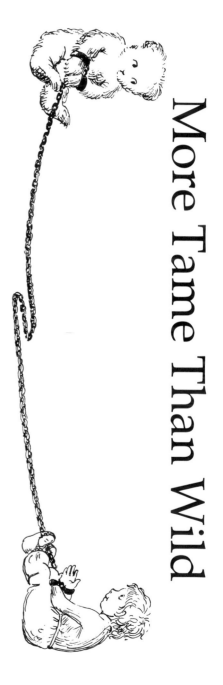

A bear on its hind legs resembles a human being. Perhaps that is why people for centuries have been amused by performing bears at markets or in circuses, menageries, or zoos. But the entertaining bear must not lull us into forgetting that bears are predators. Delight at the sight of trained bears is often mixed with terror at their strength and the savagery that can be sensed when we get too close. Is the chain strong enough? Will the bars hold? Is the pit deep enough, or can the bear jump out? Catching a bear is like conquering a piece of wilderness. It gives human beings a sense of having got the upper hand. Training a bear is yet another step in this conquest. The nose ring and chain are the visible signs of the bear's subjection. But sometimes the savagery has been retained and even reinforced by man's treatment. Bears in captivity were used in the Roman gladiator sports, and in the sport of bearbaiting, popular in England since the eleventh century. Bearbaiting, a violent and bloody spectacle, involved turning dogs loose on a chained bear. It was finally abolished in England in 1853.

From Historia de gentibus septentrionalis, by Olaus Magnus, 1555.

52

under its feet when it heard the same music, so it automatically lifted its feet.

In the 1500s, bear tamers came to Sweden from Russia and the Baltic States. In his book on Nordic peoples, first published in 1555, Olaus Magnus tells how Russian bears were tamed, by first starving them and then slowly letting them get used to the people who fed them. He says that music from flutes and trumpets inspired the bears to dance—but he says nothing about hot stones.

Some bears were also trained to carry around a hat to beg for money. If a spectator paid too little, the bear tamer made a special sign; then the bear knew it was to growl and shake its head to frighten the audience into giving more. Eventually, other animals were trained to do tricks and collect money.

Carl Peter Mazer, the Swedish painter, settled in Russia in 1838 and lived there for many years. During that time, he made a whole series of drawings of types of Russian peoples, among them the bear tamers. The stick and the chain that can be seen in the picture from the history book written in 1555 by Olaus Magnus were still being used by Russian bear tamers in Mazer's time, while the nose ring, in some cases, had been replaced by a more merciful halter. Not until World War I did the tradition of performing bears begin to die out in western Europe, although these entertaining animals still exist in the East.

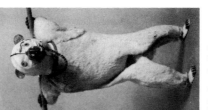

Mechanical dancing bear, Martin, France, 1903. Stockholm Toy Museum.

Circus Bears

In ancient times, the Romans built round or oval arenas in which chariot races and gladiatorial contests took place. During the modern era, the circus goes back to the eighteenth century. In 1769 in London, Philip Astley reinvented the circus ring. At first it was adapted to his own

53

Carl Peter Mazer, Russian bear showman, 1840s. National Museum, Stockholm, Sweden.

Dancing Bears

An old way of training bears to teach them to "dance." A cruel form of teaching was to force the bear to walk on hot stones or a red-hot metal plate. When it lifted it paws to get away from the worst of the heat, it looked as if it were dancing, and, meanwhile, music was played. Gradually the bear came to believe it was always hot

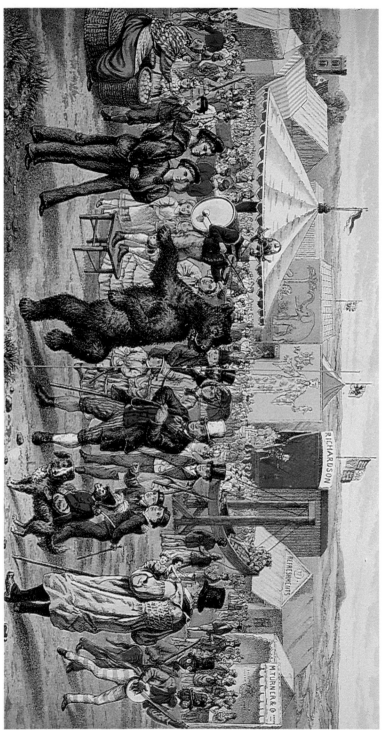

equestrian numbers, but the show was soon extended to include other artists, many of whom previously performed alone or in small groups. They now joined forces and formed circus companies with common premises. Gradually, the dancing bear was also drawn into the ring. During the nineteenth century, small and large traveling circuses became more and more common and the animals in them were the major attractions.

A second ring was not introduced until 1869, and shortly afterward James Bailey initiated the three-ring circus. Bailey merged his company with P.T. Barnum's "Greatest Show on Earth" forming Barnum and Bailey's, which was purchased by Ringling Brothers in 1907.

Today the circus has become different in different countries. The threat of

extinction and the need to protect wild life have given rise to regulations influencing the choice of circus animals. After 1960 in Sweden, it was prohibited to show wild

to share in the magical powers animals were supposed to possess. But status was also conferred on those who owned wild animals, preferably dangerous or rare ones, and unusual species were much appreciated gifts among royalty.

In 1685, a polar bear arrived in Stockholm as a gift from the Russian czar to King Karl XI. The king was interested in animals and even as a boy had his own little zoo in the Royal Palace park, with places for dogs, hares, lynx, bears, and other animals. The polar bear was called *Ursus Aquaticus* (the Water Bear) because it liked being in the water so much. It lived on Helgeland Isle in a little wooden house, where it was fastened to an extra long chain so that it could go swimming.

A rarity of this kind naturally had to be immortalized. The Swedish court painter, David Ehrenstrahl, placed the bear in its native habitat, an arctic land with steep rocky coasts, but without all the ice and snow that should be there for the illusion

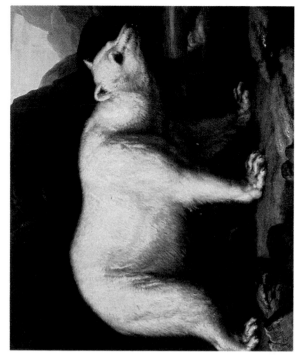

Polar Bear, David Klöcker Ehrenstrahl, 1686. National Museum, Stockholm, Sweden.

55

animals at circuses, bears included. In the Soviet Union, on the other hand, the tradition of performing bears persists, including, among other specialties, cycling bears and ice hockey games between bear teams. In the United States the circus tradition has also remained quite strong. Ringling Brothers Barnum and Bailey Circus still features many animal acts, as do other smaller traveling and local shows.

Rare Animals

As long ago as several thousand years B.C., wild animals were kept in captivity—in Egypt, for instance, and in India, where they lived in royal gardens. People wanted to find out how tame animals could become. They also hoped

From Bernie the Baby Bear, *by Erich Tylinek, 1958.*

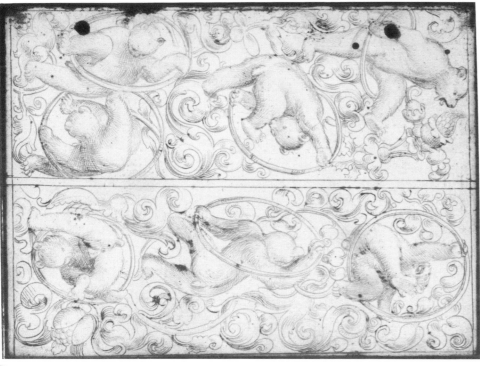

Seven Bears Leaping in Hoops, Niklaus Manuel Deutsch, c. 1519. Public Art Museum, Basel, Switzerland.

to be complete. In the painting, he also gave the lonely bear of Stockholm two friends swimming in the water.

From Bear Pit to Zoo

Legend has it that Duke Berchtold of Zähringen founded the town of Bern, Switzerland in 1911 on the exact spot where he had shot a bear. So the town got its name from the German word for bear—Bär. The bear became the symbol of the town, then eventually was incorporated in its coat of arms.

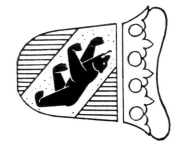

Bern (Switzerland) coat of arms. High up on its pole, the bear looks out over Bern. From St. Nicholas, 1887. Illustrator Harrison Weir.

At the beginning of the sixteenth century, the artist Niklaus Manuel Deutsch lived in Bern. He made a drawing of bears that in 1513 had been taken as spoils of war from the French. The animals had their own little house in the city's famous bear pits, the beginning of the city's famous bear pits, which still exist today. Deutsch's little rough-haired bears have soft round shapes and look almost like teddy bears as they play with hoops among luscious leafy trees.

Bear pits and private menageries are the forerunners of today's zoological gardens. The oldest zoo in existence today is in the park of the Schönbrunn Palace outside Vienna. It was founded in 1752 as a private zoo for Emperor Josef II, but in 1765 was opened to the public, in an attempt by the emperor to spread knowledge of natural history. Many of his ideas were radical for their time, and there were no direct imitators among his equals. Instead, it was the French

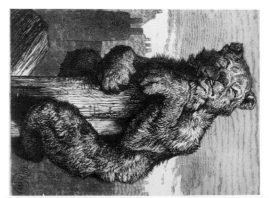

Revolutionists who put into effect this idea, when in 1793 they transferred the animals from the Palace of Versailles to the Botanical Gardens in Paris. That zoo still exists, under the name Jardin des Plantes.

Thirty years were to go by before the next large zoo was started. The London Zoological Gardens in Regent's Park were founded in 1828. Most cities soon followed London's example, and by the end of the century, there were a hundred or so public zoological gardens in the world. One reason for this was the increasing interest in natural history, and the gardens were often owned by zoological societies. At the same time, the zoo could serve as a visible reminder of the colonizing of Africa and Asia, a living proof of civilization's superiority over wild life.

Going to the zoo became a popular entertainment, and a great many zoos were set up with the aim of making money

from the spectators. This concept stimulated new ideas when it came to showing the animals. Cages were abandoned for more and more natural environments, which of course also occurred out of consideration for the animals. When Hagenbeck built his great zoo in 1907 outside Hamburg, he created artificial landscapes for his animals. With a cautious start in the 1920s, after World War II, zoos where animals roamed freely around large areas became common. A continuation of this development is the organized safari of today, in which the tourist visits the animals in their own environment.

Zoos gave ordinary people the opportunity to study at close quarters wild animals from all over the world. We even have a zoo to thank for Teddy Bear, as the zoo was where Richard Steiff's interest in bears was first aroused. Visiting zoological gardens is still a popular outing today, although television

From Chi Chi, The Bamboo Bear, by Heine and Use Demmer, 1960. Demmer brought Chi Chi to the London Zoo from China in 1958—the first giant panda to come to the West for almost twenty years.

57

58

To the garden wandered
so cheerfully,
Little Ellen and Oscar
and Frederic and me.
To the Zoological Gardens
an amazing place.
You can't visit there
without a smile on your face!

From At Skansen with Per and
Stina, by Mai Lindman, 1943.

Karin Almgren, aged 4, remembers Skansen's bears as large and horrible..

and telephoto lenses have enabled us to get close to wild animals in quite a different way. Yet seeing them on the screen, either motion picture or television, is not the same as actually being eye to eye with a bear or a lion, smelling its scent, and hearing it roar or growl.

At a zoo, we can become acquainted with animals safely, in a risk-free environment. One literally looks down on the bears that are closest. They become funny creatures standing on their back legs begging for food or rolling about on the ground. There is a risk, however, that we may be led astray into thinking the bear is just there to amuse us, and forget that adult bears can be dangerous.

Even if most children cling delightedly to the railings of the bear habitat, there are

sure to be some who sense that this hairy creature conceals a threat, so then it feels safe to hold an adult's hand. If a bear must be hugged, it's probably best if it's a teddy bear.

Once a year, Stockholm's teddy bears have a great opportunity to get to know their ancestors. When the new live bear cubs are let out for the first time, entrance to Stockholm's Skansen Park is free to anyone who has a teddy bear in his or her arms. The first day of spring in the open air and the naming of the new bear cubs is one of the traditional events in many zoos. Since the 1950s, Skansen's bears have been named after an annual alphabetical order, and anyone under fifteen years of age is allowed to make suggestions for names.

Annie and Teddy

Great big Teddy lumbers 'round his cage.
He seems rather sad, with no sign of rage.
And Annie has a pretzel she'd like to share—
"Would that please you, you great big bear?"

The heavy great bear lumbers toward the bars.
"Now, big Teddy, you can thank your lucky stars!
A pretzel is a wonderful thing to munch,
And you're going to have one for your lunch!"

Great big Teddy sits down to eat.
He seems to enjoy his little treat.
And Annie tugs at Auntie's hand—
"He's the happiest teddy in all the land!"

From *Mariae Nyckelpiga's (Ladybird's) Song Book*, by Anna Maria Roos, 1901. Illustrated by Stina Beck-Friis.

60

Teddy held tight onto Andy Pandy. "Wouldn't you like to be a real bear?" asked Andy Pandy. "No," said Teddy. "I'd much rather be your little teddy bear." From Andy Pandy at the Zoo, by Maria Bird, 1958

Eva Nordenson, director of Skansen, with Lina and Lufs in her arms, 1985.

Zoos in the United States

In the 1800's most American zoos were in the form of small menageries that toured the country, such as the exhibition by Grizzly Adams of his bears and other animals in San Francisco and New York. These attracted so much interest that cities were prompted to establish permanent zoos as public attractions in their city parks. Chicago's Lincoln Park Zoological Garden began in this way with the purchase of a young bear and four swans in 1874. In the same year, the first large city zoo opened in Philadelphia. The early zoos were generally for entertainment only and, although they may have started out with enough room, became overcrowded as they began to add more and more specimens for the public amusement. The supply of animals seemed unlimited and they were not always given the proper care. Also, as attendance increased, more room was needed for walkways and other public areas.

Toward the end of the nineteenth century, with the opening of the Bronx Zoo in New York and the San Diego Zoo in California, a new era in zoo-keeping began. Beyond mere amusement, its purposes included scientific study, education, and conservation.

A small zoo in Central Park in New York City had already been in existence since 1861, but a more spacious zoo was deemed necessary. The City of New York and the Zoological Society joined forces and opened the Bronx Zoo in 1899. The zoo, with collections that emphasize breeding groups rather than single animals or pairs, has become important in research and conservation. Two notable exhibits, Wild Asia and the World of Birds, are among the best of their kind,

In modern animal parks, the polars bears have plenty of space and swim among artificial ice floes.

In early zoos bears were generally confined to pits or small cages with little room for exercise. They were also encouraged to beg for food, which may have entertained the people but was very bad for the bears. The varying needs of different kinds of bears were not understood. In 1919 the St. Louis Zoological Society began construction of barless dens utilizing realistic concrete rockwork—the first dens of their kind in this country. Today, good zoos provide suitable environments for their bears. Polar bears, for example, are given large pools in which to keep cool and plenty of space for exercise. Formerly, female polar bears in captivity would often kill their cubs. Scientists discovered that the mother bear requires privacy since, in the wild, the female bear builds an isolated den for cubbing and remains there for several months to protect the cubs from the male bear, who will attack any newcomer—even cubs. Once the zoos provided the mother bears with quiet dens, the problem was solved.

The San Diego Zoo was an outgrowth of the 1915 California Exposition. Its stated purpose was "protecting, studying and exhibiting wild animals." Since 1922 it has been located in Balboa Park with about 5,500 animals of 1,600 different species mostly kept out in the open behind low walls or moats. Linked to the Zoo is the San Diego Wild Animal Park in the San Pasqual Valley which opened in 1973. There, the animals are maintained in as natural an environment as possible on a 1,800 acre preserve.

combining education, entertainment, and esthetic pleasure. Wild Asia is divided into a series of exhibit areas, each reproducing a different Asian habitat and containing the animals and plants natural to it.

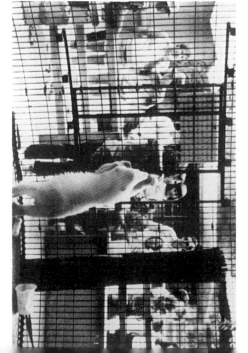

A bear's view of visitors, seen through the bars of its cage in a mor[e] traditional zoo.

Bear and People,
Ulrika Eleonora, 1682.
National Museum,
Stockholm, Sweden.

simply wants to play. Although the landscape is not entirely realistic, the houses, the people, and the bear are probably true to life.

The Bear Hunter's
Return, Adolf
Tidemand, 1858.
Detail. Gothenberg Art
Museum, Sweden.

Bears as Pets

Bear cubs captured after hunts often went to zoos. But before zoos existed, the cub might have become a pet in a family with an interest in animals. Since shooting a little bear could not be considered particularly brave, it was felt to be more "sporting" to try to teach it to be useful—as a guard bear, for instance.

Royal tame bears have been known for centuries. Some Roman emperors kept bears as pets in their households. Karl XI, the Swedish king, was a keen hunter, often moving from one palace or royal estate to another to find the best hunting grounds. His favorite place was an estate where the royal family lived in simple wooden houses, close to nature and animals. There were both elk and a tame bear on the estate. Queen Ulrika Eleonora painted a lintel on which it can be seen that the little bear has gotten free and is trying to frighten the people of the court. The maidservant with the child is taking it calmly, perhaps aware that the bear

63

In 1857, while Karl XV of Sweden was still the crown prince, he was given a pair of bear cubs as a present. A drawing by Fritz von Dardel in 1858 depicts a scene from the life of the bears. The crown prince and a uniformed keeper are exercising the bears, who are on heavy chains, in the palace park. The crown princess and their seven-year-old daughter keep a cautious distance. Nordic Museum, Stockholm, Sweden.

A Tame Bear

There are many eighteenth-century descriptions of tame bears. The fact that it was not all that easy to turn a bear into a dog but that it was a worthwhile effort is attested to by Gustaf Schröder, a noted huntsman and great author of many descriptions of hunts. In his book *Memoirs of My Hunting Life* (1899), he tells of his tame bears, and most of all about his faithful friend, Teddy.

"At last in the winter of 1865 in the month of February, I managed to take a pair of small bear cubs from hibernation, a male and a female. The poor wretches shrieked pitifully, presumably from cold, because after they had been wrapped up in a sheepskin they fell silent.

"The man who had carried them all day heard them whimpering several times and thought they were hungry. So we heated some milk, poured a little into the fingers of my reindeer skin gloves, then made a hole in them and had the glove finger serve as a nipple. This was not very successful at first, for the little hole soon got blocked, but after we had heated an

64

"awl and with that burned some bigger holes, things went well. To make the illusion as complete as possible, the cubs were wrapped in their mother's pelt overnight, after which they stayed quiet for three or four consecutive hours; then were given more milk.

"Several days went by before I got back to Siknäs, where the cubs were handed over to the housekeeper who was instructed to give them the best possible care.

"After having been away for a couple of weeks, I was back at Siknäs, curious to see my bears. The male was very ill by then. He had grown thin, and clearly he was not long for this world. The female, on the other hand, was plump and exuberant, had grown, and looked healthy. Despite everything, they had not been well cared for. Their bedding was wet and smelled badly, and they themselves were dirty. The first thing I did was to ask for them to be cleaned up and given clean, dry bedding."

Schröder goes on to relate how the little male cub dies and when he examines the bear, he finds the animal had a broken thigh bone. The remaining cub, the female, was called Teddy, and interestingly—was referred to by Schröder as *he*. It was better cared for and was washed every day. Yet "housebreaking" turned out to be difficult.

"Cleanliness was not of the best, and that was where we had our greatest struggle. He passed his water immediately, giving us no time to get him outside; but when it came to excrement, he started walking backwards, and so it was easy to eject him. He did not enjoy being out on his own, and shrieked so loudly we had to bring him in."

Teddy was a gregarious animal. He sought out people on the estate and was often given tidbits of food. Sometimes he played with the dogs. When winter came, Teddy went into hibernation, and the following April, out he crept again. When he emerged, he also had to be redomesticated. Food was put out for him, and Teddy soon made his way to the houses. He liked the brewhouse best and became a good friend to an old woman who lived there. Then he moved into an old woodshed. Schröder took Teddy with him on walks to the heath where there were plenty of anthills. They also walked in the forest and looked for berries. Teddy's love of berries once led him to look too far down in the jar. Schröder tells the story, which brings to mind both *Winnie-the-Pooh* by A.A. Milne and *Emil in Lönneberga* by Astrid Lindgren (the story of a small boy who gets his head stuck in a jar).

"The larder door had been neglectfully left open. Teddy, a great opportunist, slipped inside and among other things found a copper jar containing jam. He at once pushed his nose into it and started eating. As the contents were reduced, his head went further and further down into the jar, where it finally stuck and he could not get it out again on his own. Meanwhile I heard a peculiar subdued sound and cries and shrieks of maid servants. Sensing that something was wrong with Teddy, I hurried down to the kitchen, where I was confronted with a tragicomic scene. In a corner of the larder I saw an extremely agitated Teddy trying desperately to free himself from the jar with his front paws. However, it was stuck so firmly that all attempts, accompanied by angry grunts, were utterly fruitless. The comical aspect of the scene predominated, and I would like to have let Teddy alone for a while, but the kitchen servants were protesting so loudly, I found myself called upon to put an end to the scene as quickly as possible. So I hurried over to Teddy and very carefully tried to pull the jar off his head, but it seemed impossible. I had to use all my strength, pulling so hard that I lifted Teddy quite a distance off the floor before I at last managed to release him. But then he showed himself in all his glory up to the ears in jam. He had never had such an anointing before, and my dear Teddy was looking considerably embarrassed. The laments of the servants were replaced by peals of laughter, which made Teddy lower his head even further. It was clear that he was deeply ashamed. He beat a retreat out into the yard, where a couple of pails of cold water soon reestablished his self-respect and thus his good humor."

"Teddy contributed a great deal to the delights of home," Schröder writes. "The farm people liked playing with him, and when they had guests, Teddy had to show his tricks and be given some sweetmeat. He was very fond of punsch (a sweet liqueur) and toddy, and then wanted a wrestling match for fun. But Teddy could also take revenge if he felt insulted. He once flattened a coffee pot from which he had happened to pour boiling water over himself, and another time he punished a man who had driven him out.

"Teddy was lying asleep under the desk in the office, where Liljegren, the bookkeeper, had his place. But Liljegren

was troubled by the heat and smell that rose from Teddy, so pushed him out. Teddy resigned himself willingly to this, but when the door was not closed and Liljegren remained seated at his place at the desk, Teddy soon came back, ran through the office straight up to Liljegren's room and up onto a sofa. From there he swiped one paw at Liljegren's washing bowl so that pieces flew in all directions, then ran out again. The whole action was carried out with incredible speed. We all burst out laughing and our amusement increased when we saw Teddy standing on his hind legs with his nose pressed to the window and his eyes fixed sharply on L., as if he wished to say: 'You just leave me in peace next time!'"

Teddy was allowed to stay with the family for a few more years. In the end they were obliged to shoot him, because he frightened people who did not know him. He once playfully threw down a little girl, after which Schröder did not dare keep the bear.

"A tender farewell was taken of Teddy with a powerful hug, and after that I never again saw this son of the wilderness who had been my friend for so long."

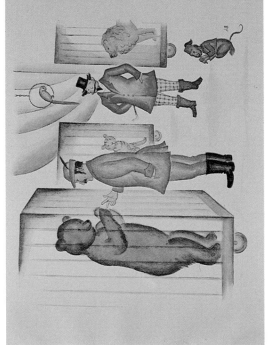

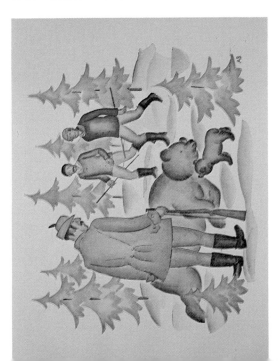

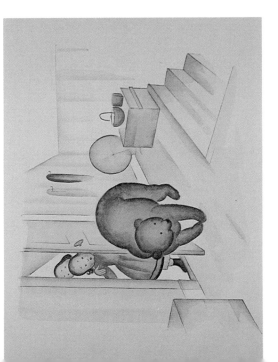

Teddy is the name of a small bear cub who grew up in a farming community in Dalarna, Sweden. When her mother was shot, she was looked after by a forester and lived in an old dog kennel. The children in the village had great fun with Teddy. But when she grew bigger and stronger, she could wrench off the chain she was fastened to. Many people were frightened and wanted her to be shot, but she was sold to a menagerie instead. This happened in the 1860s. One of the girls on the farm used to tell the story of Teddy and her exploits to her children and her grandchildren. Her daughter Märta Tamm-Gölind, published the picture book, The Saga of Teddy, *in 1926, with illustrations by Annie Bergman.*

The Bear in Children's Literature

Teddy Bear is dragged to play
in all that noise and hiphooray.
They're playing frogs—honk honky-dee—
And "The Bear's Asleep."—Oh, not for me!
To sleep in all those shouts and shocks!
Do they think I am made of rock?
They read "Three Little Bears" all through.
Ugh, so silly, it makes one spew!

From Teddy's Poetry, by Britt G. Hallqvist, 1975.

The bear is an extraordinarily cherished animal in children's literature. It has been included from the very beginning in fables, sagas, and books of facts, but not until the 1900s had it become so common that it could compete with the cat in popularity. Naturally, this occurred because the image of the bear has been reinforced by his popular relative, the teddy bear.

Facts about Bears

Children's literature in many respects follows what is happening in the adult world. When natural history began to be studied in a more scientific way in the eighteenth century, young readers were also given nonfiction books about nature. Right up to the middle of the nineteenth century, children read about bears primarily for knowledge: What species existed? What did they look like? Where did they live? What did they eat? The authors did not forget to say that the bear was a predator and that it was hunted. It was also important that the bear was represented as correctly as possible.

During the second half of the nineteenth century, knowledge started being given to children in a more easily digested form. Facts were tucked away in stories, in which individual bears were given names and were the central characters. How a bear is captured and then ends up in a zoo or a circus could become a whole book. The bear was still drawn as zoologically correct as possible, and its strength and predatory characteristics were emphasized. A bear was not something to play with. Personification of the bear even in factual books has continued to this day.

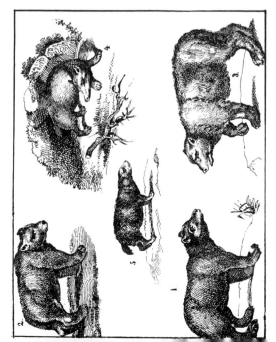

From Orbis pictus or The Visible World, 1838.

Bamse and his sister, Mova, climb trees while their mother munches berries in the marsh. Bamse Brown Bear, by Inga Borg, 1961.

The Good Bear

Throughout the nineteenth century, the bear became more and more harmless. In 1829, the Norwegian author Mauritz Hansen wrote *Little Alvhilde*, a story about a peaceful bear. In the story, some children are picking berries in the forest.

Four-year-old Alvhilde gets left behind, falls asleep, and is awakened by a growling bear eating up the contents of her basket. At first she is afraid, but then she looks into the bear's nice, kind blue eyes and realizes it isn't dangerous. Little Alvhilde is the innocent child, whose pure heart and endearing naiveté transform

69

Ollie in the Forest

Mother's little Ollie
into the forest went—
Roses on his cheeks,
and a smile from Heaven sent.
His lips are stained with berries
picked along the way.
"If only I found a friend,
I wouldn't be lonely today."

Brrm, Brrm, Brrm,
who's crashing through the wood?
The bushes crackle and bend
"A great big dog! Oh, good!"
His coat is very hairy
and his teeth are long and white.
But Ollie says, "Good morning, friend,"
with obvious delight.

Patting the bear,
with hands so small,
Ollie holds out the basket
with no fear at all.
The bear gobbles up
almost all that is there:
"Goodness me," laughs Ollie. "Berries
must be your favorite fare."

When Mother saw them together,
She let out a mighty scream.
The bear dashed away at once—
vanishing like a dream.
"Oh, Mother, why did you frighten
my new friend away?
Mother dear, please beg him
to come back again to play!"

From *Mother's Little Ollie* by Alice Tegner, 1902.
Illustrated by Elsa Beskow.

70

SUNDAY
This Little Bear Goes to Church.

Malin's Midsummer, by Mollie Faustman, 1910.

the savage animal into an equally gentle one. This romantic view of children first arose at this time, but not until the end of the nineteenth century did it become general. Then, the motif of a friendly relationship between a child and a bear became very common. Sometimes the child is shown riding on the bear, which may even have bridle and reins like a horse. The child's goodness is also put to the test on occasion. In *Malin's Midsummer* by Mollie Faustman (1910), Malin gives away her clothes to animals that are cold. But the inhabitants of the forest repay the gifts and, dressed in new clothes, she rides home on a bear. Once they are home, fruit juice and cake are set out and the bear is allowed to sit at the table. To be on the safe side, however, the party takes place outof-doors.

Even if the bear has become fairly civilized, it is still not regarded as really housebroken, nor is it allowed to sit on a stool or chair, like the dog and the cat.

The most unmitigated propaganda song about the goodness of the bear was first printed in 1902 in Alice Tegner's songbook, *Mother's Little Ollie*. "Oh, a friend, that's good. Good day to you!" cries little Ollie, a twentieth century brother of little Alvhilde. By the time the wild bear became a toy bear, children had—in stories, songs, and pictures— learned to regard it as a friend.

Industrialization changed our view of reality even with regard to animals. Where there had been forest and wild life before, now towns and other buildings grew up. The bear was no longer out hunting prey but was a harmless and cheerful figure that children could laugh at, at the circus or the zoo. The fact that it had once been regarded as strong and dangerous was now just a faint memory,

so it was not at all strange that children started hugging its image and letting it take part in the games of the nursery.

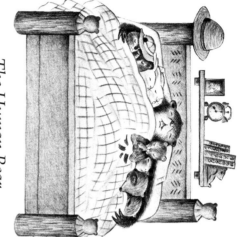

The Human Bear

The bear was humanized long ago. In fables, bears spoke and carried out human tasks. In animal stories, bears became even more like humans—wearing clothes, having a family, living in a house, and even throwing parties.

Many of the fictional bears do not lose contact with wild life completely. They often remain in the forest, and if they live in houses, then these dwellings are of

sturdy timber with rustic interiors. The furniture is made of planks and branches and textiles are home-woven in checks or stripes. Sturdy pottery mugs and plates crowd the shelves. The more the bear retains of its bear identity, the more the home resembles a forest cabin. However, the portraits of ancestors that are hung on the walls are often of real bears.

Wild bear portraits are also to be found on the walls of the more "civilized" bears that have moved into town. Their dwelling is apt to be old-fashioned and bourgeois, with a lot of small tables and ornaments. Mr. Bear in town wears a suit, whil Mr. Bear in the forest is casually dressed. The Mrs. Bears are more like each other, and wherever they live, practically always wear long skirts.

Mr. Bear is hardly ever found in a work situation. At home he is liable to be sitting and reading the *Daily Bear News*. Even when humanized, the bear prefers berries and honey, and nature's own larder presumably supplies the bear family with everything they need. But the food is prepared, and Mrs. Bear does that.

Some bears keep up with the times. In books about Victor the Bear and Josephine the Mouse, Gabrielle Vincent describes another family pattern. Josephine is Victor's "child," and he looks after her with love and care. Victor combines in himself features usually regarded as male and female. In clothing and appearance, he is undoubtedly a man, but he carries out tasks traditionally assigned to women. This unusual family situation is also remarkable in that the home is more untidy at Victor's and Josephine's than in other bear families. In fact, it has the look that is quite common in the homes of families with children.

May We Sleep Here? by Tan and Yasuko Koide, 1985 (1981). The rustic Wild West ideal leaves traces even with Japanese bears.

Victor and Josephine Lose a Penguin, by Gabrielle Vincent, 1981.

The Bear Who Wasn't a Bear, by Frank Tashlin, 1946.

wrongs the animal. Thus, anyone wishing to show solidarity with animals allows the dog to be a dog and the bear a bear.

On the bear's side is Frank Tashlin in *The Bear Who Wasn't a Bear* (1946). In this tale, everyone, even the bears in the zoo and at the circus, maintains that the bear who wakes up after his winter sleep in a newly built factory is not a bear but a stupid, lazy and unshaven fur-clad man. In the end, the bear accepts that he is a human being and meekly stands by the machine. When autumn comes and the factory is closed, he doesn't go into hibernation but, freezing cold, wanders around in the snow until instinct drives him to find his old winter quarters. Fundamentally, he is not a stupid man, but a wise bear.

The Hungarian artist and author, Janosch, has published several illustrated books about bears. By pretending to be a bear, the boy in the book *I'm a Hairy Bear* (1972), plucks up the courage to do what he is afraid to do.

"I'm telling you, you're a bear," Janosch, 1977.

73

Burre-Busse's New Clothes, by Cyrus Grané, 1948. Illustrated by Louis Moe.

Solidarity with the Bear

The great depicter of bears in Scandinavian children's literature is the Norwegian artist Louis Moe, who lived from 1857 until 1945. Although his bears have clothes, they never lose their zoological character or leave the forest or arctic regions where they belong. They always enjoy the greatest respect from the other animals. Moe wrote a great many tales about bears. In his illustrations of Cyrus Granér's book about the boy Burre-Busse's adventures among animals in many countries, the boy and the animals meet on the same level.

About the time that Moe stopped, the American Richard Scarry began drawing bears and other animals. Scarry's bears, however, live entirely human lives, the point being that in his bears we can see ourselves and our own way of life. However, pretending that an animal is a human being, some think, fundamentally

The Three Bears. *Picture books for small children,* 1869. Illustrated by Harrison Weir.

Father Ruff, Mother Muff and Little Tusse, by Aina Stenberg-Masolle, 1941.

Respect for the bear as a bear is clearer in books for young people. In the 1930s, for instance, Niels Meyn published a great many books about bears, in which the bear asserts itself against man. A truly friendly relationship between a bear and a human being is described in *Grisjka and His Bear,* by René Guillot (1959). In this and other similar books, the child takes the bear's side and defends his friend against attacks from adults.

The Appearance of the Bear

When the bear became a toy, this also influenced our perception of the bear as a good creature. The bear began more and more to be depicted as a teddy bear, its

head, ears, eyes, indeed its whole figure becoming rounder. Canine teeth and claws disappeared.

More and more books came to be written about bear cubs. This occurred probably not just because children like young animals, but also because the bear cub, with its big head and round body, looks like a real teddy bear. Both the bear cub and the teddy bear it is holding can almost be drawn identically.

A good example of the changed attitude to the bear can be found in the famous folktale about *Goldilocks and the Three Bears.* There have been many versions, but the most commonly known one is as follows.

Goldilocks is a little girl who loses her way in the forest. She comes to a house

74

and goes inside. No one is at home, but there are three bowls of porridge on a table. Goldilocks tries sitting on one of the chairs at the table, but only the third—the smallest—fits her. She tastes the food in the two larger bowls but eats the contents of the third. Then she grows tired, finds three beds, and sleeps in the littlest one, which is just the right size for her.

When the bears come home, they are upset that someone has sat on their chairs, eaten their food, and lain in their beds—*yes, indeed, is still lying there!* Goldilocks is awakened by the noise, spies the three bears, and, terrified, jumps out of the window. The child has intruded into the kingdom of the bears and is driven out of it.

Over the years, the story has changed with the bears becoming more and more friendly and harmless. In the earliest books, the bears look as menacing as they behave. They roar with loud voices. But in Aina Stenberg-Masolle's illustrated book, *Father Ruff, Mother Ruff, and Little Tusse* (1941), the bears have considerably more good-natured appearances. When Goldilocks climbs out of the window, the bear family are both disappointed and sad: Why didn't she stay and play with little Tusse?

In Kerstin Frykstrand's version in 1941, it is the bears who are frightened and jump out of the window. Goldilocks is in no hurry and makes the bed before going

home. The next day she returns holding her mother's hand and carrying a kettle of soup. While the two mothers pick berries together in complete harmony, she plays with Little Bear.

In other and more recent variations of the tale, the bears are so gentle that Goldilocks even kisses their noses. The home environment follows smoothly in

Goldilocks and the Three Bears, *by Tony Ross, 1976.*

the transformation and corresponds to the gentleness of the bears by being even cozier.

How much the appearance of the bears and the home environment mean to the character of the story becomes clear in the English author Tony Ross's horror story of 1976. Although they still live in the forest, the bears are white polar bears and that makes them even more dangerous as

Three nice, hairy, teddy-bearlike bears from the 1960s from Goldilocks and the Three Bears.

they rear up on the pages. When with all their claws and teeth they stare at Goldilocks in bed, they look like sharp saw blades. No wonder Goldilocks' hair stands on end! The polar bears live in a house with modern decor and contemporary art on the walls. Little Bear's room is full of war games and on the wall is a poster of Rupert Bear. The new times have caught up with the old fairy tale.

The little stories about Joli Coeur are meant to bring up children in a playful manner. With the aid of imagination, the little child is to see itself in the bear. Joli Coeur is well brought up and just mischievous enough. When he sees a washtub with clothes in it, he takes a bath. True, he is thrown out, but he laughs all the same. A clean bear is a happy bear.

It's really rather nice to be clean after a bath, thinks the little bear, Brummelman, seventy years later, in Torbjörn Egner's book *Klas Climber Mouse* (1953). In that book, the bear also lands in a washtub, and once he's there, Mother Bear takes the opportunity to scrub him clean as she sings a bath song for small bears:

Scrub, scrub, little Brummelman,
with soap and brush in a tub.
Until you're all fine and clean,
I'll just continue to rub.
Mother'll scrub, if she may,
brown legs and black little toes.
Goodness me, look how gray
these spots are on your nose.
Look this way, then I can
wipe your nose a while.
Turn your head so I can see
if I have to scrub your smile!
Scrub, scrub, little Brummelman,
with soap and brush in a tub.
No little bear in all the land
will be as clean as this cub!

Fin Bear jumps into the washtub . . . . . . and Paddington into the bathtub.

The Child as a Bear Cub and the Bear Cub as a Child

In the 1880s, the French children's magazine *St. Nicholas* had a page with a little bear cub called Joli Coeur. Joli Coeur is in the process of learning everything a little bear, or a little person, must know to be able to behave well: how to wash, greet people, eat nicely, and a lot more.

Call Me Paddington, by Michael Bond, 1958. Illustrator: Peggy Fortnum.

Having a bath can also be seen as initiation into a new life. The first thing both Michael Bond's Paddington and Gösta Knutsson's Teddy Lufs have to do when they come to their respective families is to go to the bathroom for a thorough scrubbing. But the bathtubs of today are more complicated than the old wooden bathtubs. Both Paddington Bear and Teddy Lufs cause a flood and almost drown. Saved for the second time, they are—fine and clean—ready to be absorbed as children in a human family, with pocket money and all.

No, it's not always easy to know what to do when you're a little person or a little

The Brown family help with the wash in The Little Brown Bear, 1984.

A little bear can also be good and helpful, like the French *Little Brown Bear*. In a series of about twenty books for small children by Claude Lebrun and Daniele Bour, Little Brown Bear plays with Papa, bathes, gets dressed, or hangs up the washing. Everyone in the family is round and tidy and everything happens very daintily and neatly. Everyone helps out, and the atmosphere in the family is warm.

Another sympathetic bear living in a secure family is Little Bear, described by Else Holmelund Minarek and Maurice Sendak in six books that appeared during the 1950s and 1960s. They tell of Little Bear's life as seen from the perspective of a child. Father works and Mother looks after the home along traditional lines, but what is new is that father and son have intimate contact—just as warm and tender as that between mother and son. In contrast to his parents, Little Bear has no clothes. There's no need. Without thinking about it, we see a little child in that little bear anyhow, and it seems quite natural that he's playing with a little girl.

Daddy Bear Comes Home, by Else Holmelund Minarek, 1959. Illustrated by Maurice Sendak.

From How Do I Eat It? by Shigeo Watenabe, 1983 (1979). Illustrator: Yassuo Othomo.

bear. How, for instance, do you eat an open sandwich? Or spaghetti? In some Japanese picture books by Watenabe/Othomo, we follow a bear cub through every difficulty. But however much he makes a muddle of things, he is nevertheless content.

Morning tasks in the teddy bear nursery, from Three Small Bears, by Anno Saxner, 1943.

Every morning we wash because all little teddy bears do that.

Teddy Bear as a Child

Many small bear cubs not only resemble a child, but also look like small teddy bears. The teddy bears in their turn often represent children. In *Three Small Bears*, by Anna Saxner (1943), the little teddy bears wake up in their sunny nursery. They wash, get dressed, and then spend their day just as small children do.

Children can also recognize themselves in *Teddy Bear*, by Grete Janus and Mogens Hertz, dressed in his short trousers and sitting at his little table in his little chair, drinking out of his tiny mug. But Teddy Bear is a real teddy bear who with his innocent looks and resolute

78

character arouses the warmest feelings in the reader. Children who can read can choose according to their mood to be either the teddy bear or the teddy bear's parents. No wonder this book about Teddy Bear has been loved by many children ever since it was published in 1945.

Grete Janus has also written *Bamse Bear's Toys* (1975), with illustrations by Iben Clante. Bamse Bear is more of a child than a bear. He loads up his toy train and sets off. The amusing situation arises when an animal that is a toy comes alive and plays with other animals that are toys. A teddy bear is the only thing missing in Bamse's toy box.

in a cottage near Stockholm's Skansen animal park with his parents. But tame Skansen bears the family certainly are not!

Max envies Nulle, who is allowed to live according to his own nature. At the same time, Max does everything he can to make him conform to accepted behavior. He even tries to get Nulle to start school. When Nulle refuses, the teacher explains the difference between animals and human beings. Animals neither can nor will think as we human beings do. "We probably have to do their thinking for them," the teacher explains, thus confirming that despite everything man is superior to the animal. Of course the bear is free, but what does he understand? What does he get out of life apart from playing and looking for sweetmeats?

The Bear as a Symbol of Freedom

Much of the time spent bringing up children entails teaching them to control themselves. In the process, they surrender much of their "freedom." The bear, which is after all an animal, can symbolize this freedom. In Gösta Reuterswärd's book, *Nulle Bearsson* (1944), the free lifestyle of Nulle the bear is contrasted with the more restricted existence of Max the boy. Yet Nulle is sufficiently civilized that he lives

Max and Nulle make a cake, from Nulle Nullesson by Gösta Reuterswärd, 1944.

79

In the books about Teddy Lufs and Paddington, the view of child and bear are different. Both Teddy Lufs and Paddington are willing to adapt to the world of humans. Neither longs to be back in his earlier life. When Paddington travels to his native country, Peru, it's only for a visit.

Teddy Lufs and Paddington's attempts to adapt to civilization reveal their weak sides. Our sympathy lies with the bear and we take on his unprejudiced eyes. Teddy Lufs and Paddington both end up in families where it is perfectly natural to have a bear as a member of the family. Although they behave and talk like people, they are, at the same time, bears. For instance, it's not easy to do the

Teddy Lufs, by Gösta Knutsson, 1949. Illustrated by Lisbeth Holmberg.

Corduroy, by Don Freeman, 1968.

to the nursery. In the store, Teddy is on a shelf waiting to be discovered, and it can be either a child or an adult who catches sight of him. If Teddy isn't taken straight from the shelf into someone's arms, then he has to rest in a box until he is unpacked on a birthday or at Christmas. "Where am I?" Teddy thinks. Nearly always he's in luck and arrives at the home of a nice family. Should he land up with a careless child, a better and more caring owner soon appears.

Christmas is a very special time for teddy bears. Teddy is often born into his family on that day and so is extra favored every year with presents and pats. But Christmas can also be terrible. Teddy can be spurned in favor of exciting new toys and end up forgotten in a corner. It can

Teddy's First Christmas, by Amanda Davidson, 1982.

Teddy and Anna Find New Friends, by James Stevenson, 1981.

cooking when you've got paws, but luckily most people understand bears. Only people with unyielding principles think bears make a mess and should really be sent back to the forest.

Teddy Gets His Family

A teddy bear's route to his owner can occasionally be somewhat roundabout, but usually it's straight from the toy store

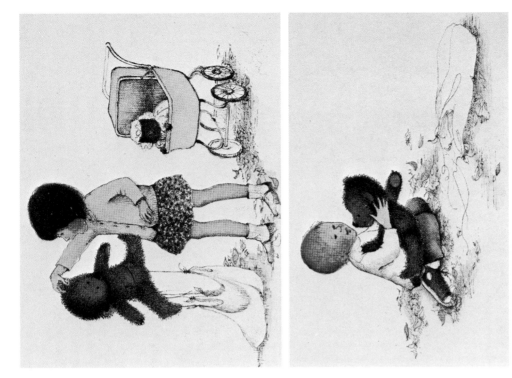

even be so terrible that Teddy ends up in the trash can. However, things almost always sort themselves out in the end for a teddy bear. If it's not a happy reconciliation with his former owner, then it's a happy association with a new one.

A Teddy Bear to Play with

Just as in real life, a teddy bear's task in children's books is to be the child's "child." He is brushed and combed, dressed, and given rides in a baby carriage.

Sometimes the teddy bear is a mute toy, but other times he comes to life. The English author Joan G. Robinson has written several books describing what it's like to be the teddy bear of a little girl, including *Dear Teddy Robinson* (1956) and *Another Teddy Robinson* (1960). Teddy Robinson is very particular about his position in the nursery. He is the one who is allowed to sleep with the little girl at night, while the dolls have to stay in their own beds. Teddy knows he is loved and feels secure.

In the book about Charles the bear (1971), Liesel Moak Skorpen tells of a bear who is at first insensitively treated by a girl and is then exchanged for a cat and ends up with a boy who understands his need for adventures as well as for quiet moments. Instead of being dragged round in a carriage, Charles goes parachuting, and when he hurts himself, is tenderly cared for. Illustrated by Martha Alexander.

In most books about children's games with teddy bears or bears, the girls have a mother-child relationship with the teddy, while boys see him as a friend. Together with boys, the teddy bear can join in a great many exciting adventures.

81

*It's better
to be a bear
than a bubble!
From Teddy Robinson
by Joan G. Robinson,
1961.*

Just imagine flying straight toward the stars! From Little Bear's Radio Journey Among Stars and Clouds, by Bo Vilson, 1931.

A saga, modern for its day, is Bo Vilson's *Little Bear's Radio Journey among Stars and Clouds* (1931). With a teddy bear under his arm, the boy Björn [Swedish for *bear*] presses his ear to the amazing radio set. What does it not contain? When night falls, Björn and Teddy fly through space, and high up on a cloud they are received by King Ether. It is a meeting between two saga worlds, where Teddy represents a safe and familiar world and King Ether a new and fascinating one, both equally necessary.

A girl can also take Teddy with her on adventurous journeys. Gunnel Linde's *Miss-Alone-At-Home Goes by Rocking Chair* (1963) is about the fantasy games of an only child. Together with two teddy bears, Brumbo and Littlest Teddy, Miss-Alone-At-Home sets off on the linoleum

Adventures of Teddy Bear

Teddy Bear's personality is a mixture of contentment and a desire for adventure. So Teddy liberates himself early on from the nursery and sets off into the world.

Grand Duchess Olga's Picture Book. The Adventures of Three Small Bears (1924) describes all the stages that a bear journey can have. It all starts in the nursery, where the bears sit drooping miserably because

sea, where a storm is raging and they are shipwrecked. But on her comfortable bed, she can gather her strength for new adventures and encounters with both good and evil creatures. Miss-Alone-At-Home is strong and brave. She comforts the teddy bears in difficult moments, but they also share the delights of playing together. They are both children and playmates.

Miss Alone-At-Home, Brumbo, and Littlest Bear are building a wall with bricks so that no one from the outside world can come and disturb their journey. From Miss-Alone-At-Home Goes by Rocking Chair, by Gunnel Linde, 1963. Illustrated by Hans Arnold.

Grand Duchess Olga's Picture Book. *The story of three bears and their adventures, with verses by Margit Ekegardh, 1924. Grand Duchess Olga was sister of the last Russian Czar, Nicholas II, and daughter of the Danish princess Dagmar. The Grand Duchess lived in Denmark in the 1920s.*

they have been spurned by their owner in favor of a building blocks set. They decide to run away, and with the help of a basket and three balloons, they construct a craft that carries them out of the window. After the balloons get stuck in a tree, the bears enjoy life in the wilderness. But when autumn comes, it's good to find their way back home.

Sometimes there is something that drives bears away from home. In the 1930s, the Finnish author, Margit von

83

Teddi, drawn by Signe Hammarsten-Jansson, 1934.

Teddy Goes to Timbuctoo, by Mollie and Patrick Matthews, 1975.

Willebrand-Holmérus, wrote two books about her daughter's soft toys. In *Sly Furry Creatures* (1936), all the animals go around the world to visit their relatives, including traveling to Greenland, where Teddi was born as a polar bear. As a teddy bear, Teddi also enjoys polar bear food:

Snow and ice
brrrm brrrm
ice and snow
brrrm brrrm.
Isn't it nice
brrrm brrrm
to hear the wind blow
brrrm brrrm.

Meat and fat
brrrm brrrm
fat and meat
brrrm brrrm.
I say that
brrrm brrrm
is good to eat
brrrm brrrm.

Another Finnish-Swedish author, Solveig von Schoultz, has used her daughter's toys as the main characters in a book called *Teddy Bear's Journey* (1944).

During World War II, thousands of Finnish children were sent to Sweden, Solveig von Schoultz's two daughters among them. In *Teddy Bear's Journey*, the girls' "children"—their dolls and teddy bears—make the same trip on their own. Elsie the doll keeps a watchful eye on the company and has quite a time keeping track of them all, not least Teddy Ivan and Teddy Steven.

The English Teddy Edward is a real explorer. His adventures are told by Mollie Matthews and are illustrated with photographs taken by Patrick Matthews. Teddy Edward appeared in a book for the first time in 1962, then became a famous television star in England with his own series. He skis in the Alps and visits other parts of the world. Teddy Edward is photographed in real landscapes, and we can see just how small a teddy bear is. If he can manage the Sahara, then anyone can!

A Bear That Just Is

A. A. Milne's Winnie-the-Pooh is a bear with a very small brain who nevertheless thinks and ponders quite a bit. He takes the day as it comes, lets nothing amaze him, has a solution for all problems, is a friend to his friends and a great student of life. Nothing surpasses a quiet moment with a good friend and a jar of honey.

Milne's books about Winnie-the-Pooh (the first one came out in 1926) tell the story of a little boy called Christopher Robin and his toy animals. Christopher Robin was Milne's own son and the toys were his toys. Few bears live up to Pooh's personality. He is not only a dear silly old toy bear, but a real friend who has much to offer. No one questions that Pooh is the real main character, not only in the

Illustration by Ernest H. Shepard. From Winnie the Pooh, by A.A. Milne, 1926.

Hundred Acre Wood, but also in the entire kingdom of teddy bears.

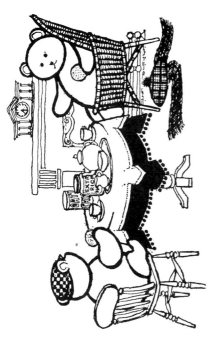

A Pleasant Home for Teddy

All independent teddy bears who have left the nursery behind have homes of their own. Winnie-the-Pooh's cozy corner with its checked tablecloth, a clock on the wall, and a shelf for jars of honey has become the prototype for the ideal interior. It is a home that reflects security and snugness, a corner for both teddy bears and children to relax in. It is a home to return to after outings, difficulties, and primitive overnight stays under field conditions.

It's pleasant for a bear to come home to the warmth of a fire, take a dollup of honey, talk to a friend, read the *Daily Bear News*, and finally creep under the patchwork quilt and sleep soundly all night.

A Bear in the Hand

In children's books, most teddies live an independent life. Many of them are little personalities, full of thoughts and feelings and special qualities. But yet, even as the teddy bear has developed its endearing personality, it has also sometimes been degraded to being a lifeless prop for small children.

In many books, children are illustrated with a teddy bear in their hands, without that having anything to do with the story. A teddy bear may lie flung down among other toys on the floor, a lifeless object among other dead things.

When the teddy bear loses his personality, he also loses shape, the border between a teddy and other animals being wiped out. Sometimes it can be quite difficult to differentiate between Teddy and a shapeless

Albert, by Alison Jezard, 1972. Illustrator: Margaret Gordon.

cushionlike object. The bear cannot be further away from its original position of respect as king of the forest kingdom and worthy opponent of man.

If in a teddy bear we can see a small child, then in an abandoned teddy we can also perceive an abandoned child. A teddy bear that is nothing but a nursery fitting can be translated into a child who is a subsidiary person in a home. However, it is not necessary to take the resemblance quite that far to establish that the treatment of the teddy bear also says something about the perception of the child. Showing respect for what belongs to the world of the child is also showing respect for the child.

But a forgotten teddy bear can take things into his own hands:

How upset they'll be when I get there!
"Did we forget you, darling bear?
We're sorry!" Then I'll say,
"That's alright!"
And we'll have a party 'til late at night!

Britt G. Hallqvist's *Teddy Bear's Poetry* (1975) is a book in which all friends of teddy bears can recognize themselves and Teddy Bear. For those who are tempted to forget that Teddy Bear is also a creature with a soul, her book is the best possible "medicine."

Four Steiff Bears Find Their Way Home

Was drei kleine Bäien im Walde erlebten (Three Little Bears in the Woods), by Margaret Thiele, 1923. Illustrator: F. Schenkel.

Pelle came to a boy called Klaus in about 1921. Ingeborg, Klaus's sister, pulled Pelle's arms about, so that he was slightly damaged. Then she took over Pelle, and her brother was given a new yellow teddy. Pelle was renamed Pellerinchen and was given girl's clothes, but all the same was still called "he." Ingeborg played with her teddy a great deal and sometimes he was given a ride in the doll's carriage in the park. Pellerinchen was very smart in a red-and-white striped dress, knitted red stockings, and a little net cap out of which the ears could protrude.

Ingeborg didn't like her afternoon nap. Instead, she made mountains and valleys out of her bedclothes, and Pellerinchen was allowed to roam there. She once cut his hair; unfortunately, it never grew again. Since then, Ingeborg has made a new fur coat for Pellerinchen several

times over, and also knitted a blue and yellow suit so that he doesn't get cold in his old age.

Ingeborg and her brothers and sisters had a great many teddy bears. Wollbäckchen came in 1931 and gradually ended up with younger sister Karin. He was already one-eyed even then. He had acquired his name from a German children's book about three bears in the forest. The children's mother came from Germany, and both the children and their bears could speak German.

Because of World War II, the family's twins, born in 1938, had to wait a long time for their Steiff bears to come from Germany. Meanwhile they made do with Swedish teddies named Uffe and Iffe. In 1946, however, Jochen and Putz arrived, and now the three bears of the book were complete. The family thinks Steiff bears are the best.

86

I Thought It Was a Moon

"Teddy Lufs!" said Lotta.

Teddy Lufs looked up. He was sitting crocheting in the rocking chair.

"Is it a question of you wanting something?" said Teddy Lufs.

"Yes, Teddy Lufs," said Lotta. "I was thinking about something, and that is that you really *must* learn to read. And do sums."

Teddy Lufs glanced away.

"But I'll be quite worn out with all that learning," he said. "I've just learned to crochet—won't that do for a while?"

"What are you crocheting, Teddy Lufs?" said Lotta.

"Reins," said Teddy Lufs.

"But you were going to crochet a potholder for Grandmother," said Lotta.

"I've changed my mind," said Teddy Lufs. "It's going to be reins instead. They could be good for Grandmother to have if she goes out for a drive. Or riding or something. She's going to have ten thousand feet of reins."

"Can you spell *reins*, Teddy Lufs?" said Lotta.

Teddy Lufs looked away.

"I expect I could, if I wanted to," he said after a while. "But I think it's so terribly *unnecessary*. The main thing is that I know they're *called* reins, isn't it?"

"Everyone has to learn to read and write and do sums," said Lotta. "Grandmother can and the trumpeter can, and I can. You're the only one who can't, Teddy Lufs."

"You see, there weren't at all that many schools in the forest where I lived before," said Teddy Lufs, screwing up his eyes.

"No, but that's why I want to teach you now," said Lotta. "Well, Teddy Lufs, how do you think you spell *reins*?"

"Q, X, Z, 37," said Teddy Lufs. "Or something like that."

"Reins begins with R," said Lotta. "Anyone can hear that."

"Can we have some toast?" said Teddy Lufs. "With honey on it?"

"Now pay attention," said Lotta. "Reins begins with R, and then comes *Eee*."

"Oh, now I understand," said Teddy Lufs. "That teeny weeny island out in the lake. Where we go for picnics and have *teeeee* and toast. with honeeeeey on it."

"This is going well," said Lotta. "I mean that you seem to understand about Eee. Now, the next letter is I. How do you spell island?"

"P," said Teddy Lufs.

"Teddy Lufs, Teddy Lufs!" said Lotta. "You must know that *island* starts with I. *I* is just like *I*, and *idea*. Every little child can hear that. How do you spell *idea*, Teddy Lufs?"

"D," said Teddy Lufs.

"Teddy Lufs, Teddy Lufs!" sighed Lotta again.

"But you said I was just like *idea*," said Teddy Lufs. "I heard that. And if *I* is like

then *idea* must start with *D*. Otherwise I don't want to learn to read."

"Let's do some writing instead," said Lotta. "Come and sit beside me, Teddy Lufs."

Teddy Lufs scrambled out of the rocking chair and sat down at the table beside Lotta.

"Look now," said Lotta. "I'll draw a straight up-and-down line with a little line at the top and at the bottom. That's an I."

"But eyes don't look like that," said Teddy Lufs. "They're round and have a circle inside them."

"You're quite hopeless," said Lotta.

"Can I draw a head around the I and then add your nose and mouth?" asked Teddy Lufs. "And a mustache?"

From Teddy Lufs on the Go, by Gösta Knutsson, 1966.
Illustrated by Lisbeth Holberg.

T. R. Arrives

It all started when Jimmy got a package from America. Since it was neither Christmas nor his birthday, the package was a surprise for everyone.

Jimmy carried the package up to his room to open it.

Everyone else was so curious that they all followed him, all the way up to his attic bedroom at the top of the tall old London house.

The whole family gathered around.

There was Jimmy's father—tall, wearing glasses, and absentminded. He taught history and wrote books that no one seemed to want to buy.

There was his mother, round and untidy and scatterbrained.

She made pots and vases and dishes in a kiln at the back of the garden.

The pottery was so strangely shaped that no one seemed to want to buy it either.

There was Jimmy's elder brother George, wearing glasses like his father, and trying to look serious and important and grown-up.

And finally his sister Jenny, younger than George but older than Jimmy, who secretly thought she was the nicest and most sensible and most really grown-up of the entire family.

Inside the box, there was a bear.

It was a teddy bear. But somehow it wasn't quite like any other bear he'd ever seen.

It was smallish and broad-shouldered.

Instead of the gentle, happy air of most teddy bears, this bear had a kind of determined, almost scowling, expression. This bear looked tough, despite the fact

that it was wearing glasses—small, perfectly round ones with black wire frames.

"Surely a bear can't need glasses," thought Jimmy.

Then he realized that the glasses had no glass in them.

There was a letter on top of the bear. Jimmy took it out of the box and handed it to his mother. "You read it, Mom."

His mother looked at the letter. "It's from your Uncle Colin in Connecticut." Jimmy's mother's brother was a history professor who had taken a job in an American university.

Jimmy's mother peered at the letter through her glasses—round ones rather like the bear's except hers were gold-rimmed. She began to read.

"Dear Jimmy,

We found this teddy bear in the attic. According to the label on the box, his name is Theodore Roosevelt Bear. That's a bit of a mouthful. You could call him T.R. for short."

Jimmy looked down at the bear.

Lying in his box of tissue paper, the bear looked rather as if it was asleep in bed.

Just to try out the sound of it, Jimmy said, "T.R. Bear!"

The bear woke up. Its eyes opened wide behind the round spectacle frames. It yawned and stretched and sat up, looking the astonished Jimmy straight in the eye.

"Hi there, kid," said T.R. Bear. "How are you doing?"

From *Enter T.R.*, by Terrance Dicks, 1985. Illustrated by Susan Hellard

The Bear Who Could Imagine

He had been forgotten. He had been forgotten. He had been quite forgotten. He had been absolutely and completely forgotten.

It was getting darker and darker in the grass where he was sitting, and there were no girls running around any more.

She would pay for this, that girl, now fast asleep in the house, that girl, Barbara, who had been given him and had forgotten him out here—she would pay for this!

That was what he was thinking as he sat there feeling like a bad bear, a really real bear, a dangerous bear, a bear used to eating meat.

Because he could imagine things. Yes, he could do that.

He imagined prowling through the tall grass. But it was horrible, and he quickly

He crossed one teddy bear leg over the other, as he sat there, and leaned back against a mound of grass.

Perhaps it wasn't necessary to imagine horrible things, he thought, unbuttoning his fur coat to feel easier. Now the stars could also shine down on his new checked vest.

He had no jacket, but anyhow there was a neatly sewn flower in every square of the vest.

Because he could imagine things like that.

He looked at the clock. It wasn't a clock, but a little sun.

He put it in the sky where it soon grew big, but it might fall down.

"Auntie!" he cried. "Madame Auntie Barbara!"

The sun rose to its proper place and shone just as it does in the daytime.

He'd imagined that marvelously.

He uncrossed his legs and said to himself, "*You* can stay sitting here, but I—*I'm* going to stand up now."

And he stood up in the sunlight.

He stood like a teddy bear gentleman, lacking only a stick.

He was already swinging his stick, because that was easy to imagine.

But now—

"Auntie!" he cried. "Auntie Barbara!"

The other one, who should have stayed

changed his mind, thinking he ought to be polite to the girl.

"Madame," he cried, "Madame Auntie Barbara!"

He imagined the whole house waking up, because of the frightening way in which he had cried out.

But the house was just as silent, so silent, as if it wasn't even breathing.

What was going to happen tonight? What could a creature shut out all alone in this tall grass do?

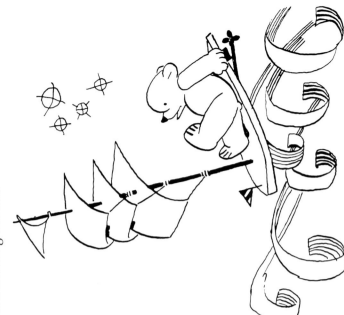

sitting there, got up on all hairy fours and growled.

"You poked me."

"I didn't mean to, little brother—no don't get so big—you must be a real . . ."

"I'm a real proper bear," growled the other one. "Because I can also imagine things!" he added. Then the bear grew so big that he hid the sun.

"Auntie!" the little teddy cried, his teddy bear heart in his throat.

He had to sit down again for a while. And when he was again sitting in the tall grass, he promised himself he would never again imagine that he was two bears.

Because that was horrible.

No, it would be better to imagine sitting there asleep. So that's what he did. Goodnight to the whole world, grass, darkness, and everything.

He sat there with one teddy bear leg crossed over the other, leaning back in a boat with a morning-red sail.

Because he could imagine things like that as he slept.

The waves were like blue velvet and carried him gently, rising and falling, rising and falling, rising . . .

"Auntie! Auntie Barbara!"

It was such a dizzily high wave he was almost frightened.

"Auntie!"

It suddenly sank as if into a chasm and he felt hollow inside.

But then he was near a green island. He grabbed a branch and hauled the boat ashore.

"Oh . . ." he yawned hugely, sleepy as anything.

A large nut was thrust into his mouth.

"Crack it!" someone said.

He cracked it. All he had to do was to bite.

But then another nut was thrust into his mouth.

"Crack it!"

He cracked it, for what could he do? There were about a hundred grinning monkeys all around him wanting to have their nuts cracked so that they needn't bother themselves.

"Crack it! Crack it! Crack it!"

He cracked and cracked the nuts, all the time thinking it would serve her right, that girl Barbara, who had forgotten him out there. For if she hadn't done that, he wouldn't have had to be a nutcracker, at least not for the monkeys.

He cracked and cracked until his jaws ached, but the little beasts just grinned and popped more nuts into his mouth. At last his patience came to an end.

"Don't imagine I'm a nutcracker," he growled so that it could be heard all over the green island, because he could imagine it doing that.

Soon all the monkeys were back high up in the tall trees. Poor scared wretches.

He walked proudly out onto the water, because he had quite enough of sailing.

He walked on the gently billowing velvet waves, sometimes on two legs, sometimes on four, because it was always rather uneven. Anyhow, there was nothing shameful about a bear walking on all fours.

Then the waves got rather worse, carrying him up, then down, but as it was all velvety gentle, it didn't matter that he sometimes came down on his nose and sometimes with the other end first.

Yes, it did get a trifle tiring scrabbling upward when the velvet wave rose almost like a wall, but downward was much easier, perhaps just a bit too easy.

It happened that he rolled down like a ball.

It happened that he tumbled down in a bundle.

It happened that he was flung between the huge velvety waves like any old thing, up onto the highest crests and down into the deepest depths, then up again, and

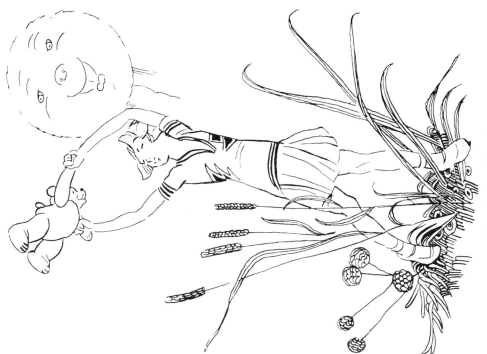

down again, incessantly, again and again, continuously.

It happened that he gave up all hope of ever getting ashore. And whose fault was that? He knew that all right.

But he wouldn't cry out now, not make a single sound, not do anything except allow himself to perish.

And when he finally went under those more and more enormous velvety billowing waves, then that girl Barbara who had left him outside, she would miss him and be bitterly sorry.

Yes, she would. He could clearly imagine that, however far gone he was otherwise.

"Auntie!"

He was flung toward the stars . . .

But before he came down again, he just had time to think that she would pay for this!

When he did come down again into the tall dark grass, he felt content with his decision to make her pay for what he had had to go through.

He crossed one teddy bear leg over the other and looked cross and determined.

But ssh! Someone was running, someone skipping, someone laughing. The girl.

Suddenly he was lifted up into the air. "Oh, you naughty little careless thing, you. Oh, you sweet little ugly creature! Oh, you silly little nitwit!"

She had found him and thrown him into the air, taken him on her arm and rocked him, spanked him and pinched him, and laughed and laughed and laughed.

And he, why didn't he reproach her now? Why didn't he feel like an angry bear, a real proper bear, a dangerous bear, a bear used to eating meat?

Well, perhaps he might imagine something else.

And he did so.

Because how could he do anything else when the girl Barbara ran and skipped and laughed and laughed and laughed.

The sunny whirlwind!

Ha, ha, he'd imagined a name for her that suited her down to the ground.

And that was all she paid for leaving him behind outside.

Because he could imagine that he had done that.

Then the sun rose. And then?

The sun rose higher. What more?

What did he care about that, he who was cross and determined?

From *The Christmas Load* by Vilhelm Nordin, published by Ahlen & Akerlund, 1931. Illustrated by Erik O. Strandman.

The Dolls Have a Bath. From Children's Christmas Present, by Brita Ellströ, 1915.

Make-Believe and For Real

Little Johnny and the Teddy Bears, by R.D. Towne. Illustrated by J.R. Bra[...]

From very early on, Teddy Bear was given a favored place in the nursery. Among other things, Teddy was allowed to sleep in bed with the children and go with them on journeys. In games on the nursery floor, other animals have nearly always had to hand over the chief role to the teddy bear, just as A.A. Milne has described in his books about Winnie-the-Pooh and his friends. Not even the fashionable animals of today have become a serious threat to the teddy bear or can push him aside from the place closest to children's hearts. This remains true even though children today may possess a dozen soft toys. The teddy bear is still of such importance that the word teddy has become synonymous with the toy children like best—whether that favorite "teddy" is a monkey or a dog.

security but also offered a stimulus for the imagination. But the teddy bear's dual task of offering security and being a confidante is just as important today. Now as then, it is just as important that Teddy goes along as a traveling companion. How many parents have not been forced to turn back home to fetch a forgotten teddy bear without whose presence the whole holiday would be ruined? And how many children refuse to go to the doctor or dentist without taking

Ready to Go. From Housewife, No. 27, 1924.

Teddy Bear as a Faithful Friend

The teddy bear is often treated as a member of the family. He takes part in all everyday activities and joins in on festive occasions. Unlike other toys, the teddy bear is not a seasonal creature. All this gives him a special position among the toys. But most important of all, the teddy can be both an inanimate object and a creature with a soul, and as such can represent both an animal and a person. This concept opens the door to a rich world of fantasy that can be shaped according to the needs of the moment.

Perhaps children used to be left on their own much more and so needed a playmate who not only provided the child

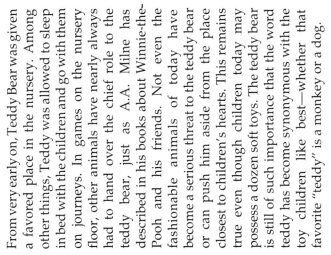

1930s bookmark

95

their beloved Teddy along firmly by the hand?

The role of the teddy bear as a safe companion is most noticeable when it's time to go to bed. In the darkness of the night, someone you can rely on is truly necessary. Even adult teddy bear owners can often remember the terrors of those nights when for some reason Teddy was not there.

It is also good to have someone who always has the patience to listen, and long into school years it is the teddy bear who has the time. It is precisely the teddy's patience that is such an important quality. He endures difficulties without complaining and is an ideal companion on outings. He likes looking at the world from a bicycle basket, listening to the wind in the treetops, or spending a night in a tent.

Teddy Bear Names

Teddy bears are usually given names—in this way, they assume an identity of their own, become Someone. Most teddy bears are simply called Teddy, but there are a great many variations—Ted, Edward, Big Bear, Bear, Big Ted, Little Ted—as well as perfectly ordinary names, fanciful names like Snowberry or Periwinkle, or names connected with the sound "Brrm" (Bruno, Brum-Brum, Brumble, and so on). Girl's names are rarer. It seems to be easier to perceive the bear as male.

Teddy Bear as Prey

In boys' games, the teddy bear can be transformed into a cowboy, Indian, Superman, or some other hero, who has one exciting adventure after another. Teddy can even be the enemy, the person the boys measure their strength against. But he can also be the prey.

Sometimes, the teddy bear turns into a really dangerous and menacing *bear*. On other occasions, with the aid of suitable attributes, the teddy bear takes on the form of another animal. A bear dressed in a "lion jersey" becomes a "lion bear," and sheltered behind some piece of furniture, his owner can fire a death-dealing shot at this unsuspecting wild animal. A teddy bear becomes what his owner wants him to be.

Teddy Bear as a Child

What makes the teddy bear so unique is that in the same figure he combines both strength and weakness. Although Teddy

Britt-Marie with homemade sheepskin bears in her bicycle basket, 1940s.

Bear protects and consoles, he also needs looking after and being cared for. In *My Teddy*, by Juliet Bawden and Helen Pask, the nighttime friend and protector assumes the role of a little child, having

Now the guests come to my ball—
Ester the doll first of all.

Then comes Miss Whizzlywise,
who can even close her eyes.

Then big Edward Teddy Bear,
he doesn't even need a chair.

easier if the imaginary child has form—a piece of wood, for instance—but even better if it has a head, arms, and legs like a teddy bear.

By acting out roles, the child develops as a human being. Teddy Bear is given roles to play, needs, skills, and other things the child has to be trained in or confront. When children fuss over their teddy bears, they are training themselves to look after people, while at the same time learning from the games that people do sometimes need taking care of. The small child is thus helped to accept his or her own smallness.

Barbro, three years old, out for a walk with Teddy, 1935.

undergone all the evening routine of a child—being washed, having his teeth cleaned, being toileted, and then being dressed in pajamas. When the bear thus becomes a child, the child becomes its thoughtful parent.

The teddy bear can also be a child in the daytime in mommy-daddy-children-games. Children of today also like to play "kindergarten"; then they are the nursery school teachers, and their dolls and bears become the nursery school children.

Teddy Bear as a Catalyst

A teddy bear is nothing much but an inanimate object made of cloth and stuffing. But he functions as a catalyst and sets the child's imagination in motion. The games go on in the child's head, but the teddy or doll is necessary so that the abstraction shall not be too great. It can be tricky trying to keep track of an imaginary friend or an imaginary child. It is much

Class 4c of Johannesbäck School in Uppsala with their favorite teddy bears. In the middle is a Björn Borg teddy bear.

So the teddy bear functions as a substitute, much the same as a doll, in the role play so necessary for human growth. But the teddy bear's range is greater than that of the doll, because he is an animal. A doll resembles a child and cannot represent just anything. A teddy bear can be anything from a nursery school child to

a pirate or a lion. A doll can be only a person. The bear offers a greater range for the imagination and also provides a certain remoteness so that the game does not risk being faithful to reality and thereby becoming inhibited.

Teddy Bear, a Companion for Life

A great many people keep their teddy bears all their lives. There is a personal relationship with teddy bears that never releases its grip. Who can forget a real friend, perhaps the only friend who really understood? The only one who could see a polar bear on the lawn or a witch in the old house in the woods? Or the only one who hugged you hard when the ghost appeared at the bedroom window? As a result, many people think more than twice before lending their teddy to anyone. There are risks involved! Imagine Teddy getting hurt, disappearing, or even simply dying! So it is often only within the

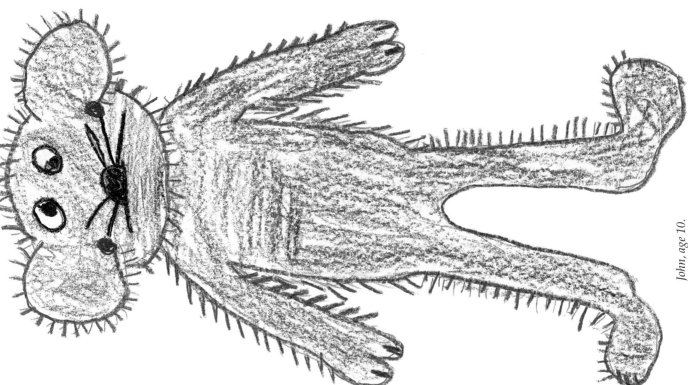

John, age 10.

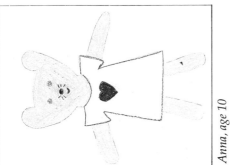

Matthew, age 10

Anna, age 10

ur walls of home that a teddy bear is
anded over to someone else's care.

Many bears have to go with their
wners through all the various moves in
fe. Sometimes, it is the only member of
ne family who stays with you all through
fe. Perhaps what a teddy bear owner
nce said is true: "A real teddy bear never
ets his owner down."

"When we play mommies, daddies,
nd children, Teddy's important. We look
fter him just as the grown-ups do. And
e take him for a walk in the doll carriage
nd make sure he doesn't get chilled if it's
old out. He might get a cold and then it'd
e too bad, and perhaps we couldn't go
ut for ages. And then we have to change
is diapers. That's important."

– Eva, age 6.

"Sometimes we go in the car to see
randmother and that's a long way away.
take my Teddy with me then. We have a
vely time in the back then, and we look
ut. I mostly have to show him, but . . .
nce he saw a dog as we drove past . . . and
hen he sort of seemed scared."

– John, age 5.

A teddy bear can be soft and nice to hug, the kind of bear that is required to be able safely to fall asleep. But a teddy bear can also be so much else—anything from an astronaut or a commando to an explorer out on an adventure, or quite simply an ordinary citizen in an advanced bear society.

Those were the teddy bears we preferred to play with, all of us boys who lived in the yellow house on Ring Road. And that was the teddy bear age, when we were in elementary school at the beginning of the 1970s.

The bears were scarcely hand-high, and it is no exaggeration to say that they had just as wonderful adventures as Selma Lagerlöf's Nils Holgersson had. Adventures in all forms were to be characteristic of the flourishing and

elevated teddy bear culture in the yellow house. The bears had many exciting adventures in the little grove of trees near our block. Courage and the joys of discovery were characteristic of our bears, who with tremendous difficulties and hardships penetrated further and further into the unexplored wilderness in order to explore and map it. Another scenario for adventures was the sand pit in the park, where there was a huge and harsh desert stretching for miles. Very few bears ever dared venture into this desert, and no one knew for sure what the country beyond it was like, but occasionally, however, there were fortune-hunting bears, who went on expeditions far into the interior of the desert.

During these voyages of discovery, the teddy bears met new people and families with strange ways and customs. The bears had a clearly pronounced defensive attitude and were keen to maintain their sovereignty and keep guard over their own territory as well as over new land conquests. The constant threat hovering over the bears came from the Dolls and the Vandals. To defend their community and their culture against these hereditary enemies, the bears mobilized a well-equipped army that was constantly on the alert.

The teddy bears, however, were fundamentally a peace-loving and harmonious tribe, who at quite an early stage had realized that conflicts could not be prevented or solved by force, but could be averted only through understanding and a firm judicial policy. On the basis of this reasoning, the bears adopted and had committed in paper what was called the

The bears in the
Yellow house force
themselves to attempt
difficult climbs.

From "The Bears
of the Yellow
House," by Erik Ronne.

Teddy Bear Law, which, in combination with a large number of verbal agreements and conventions, guided their lives. The supreme judicial authority was Little Yellow, founder of one of the clans and its obvious leader.

Architecturally, bear society was at an advanced high level. Although the first bears lived their strenuous lives in shoe boxes and dirty holes in the ground, more advanced and imaginative architecture was to become a characteristic of teddy bear culture. In time, the bears not only became masterly at building the simple but aesthetically perfected bear tent of sticks and moss, but also built a number of more advanced complexes and monuments, especially in the sand pit.

After a heavy rainfall, the sand pit was also an excellent place for the bears to practice their skills at the technique of constructing highways and water installations. An odd deviation of architectural delight was the creation called the Hamster Cake—a kind of Knossus in miniature. The name

stemmed originally from the labyrinths in, with a large number of... Lego built by big brother for the family's hamsters.

A measure of civilization is the art of writing. It has been established that this art was not entirely known to the teddy bears, but was largely limited to maps of treasure and secret messages hidden under doormats. However, at one time, a magazine regularly came out called the *Teddy Bear Chronicle*. This was primarily intended as a newspaper with topical reportage, but it also contained a touch of a weekly, with contributions of humor and ghost stories. Sometimes it also functioned as an organ for the publication of buying and selling on the stock exchange.

We boys in the yellow house learned the art of social structure with the bears. We encapsulated ourselves within the architecture and acquired the basics of conventional warfare. It was fun!

War

Suddenly the sirens wailed in this otherwise calm and peaceful little settler community of bears. A cloud of dust on the horizon indicated that heavy armored divisions of the Dolls in Lego were swiftly advancing across the grass. The veteran bears hurried to group in defense positions around the town in order to open counterfire against the approaching enemy. The battle was fierce, and despite a massive barrage from the defenders' bunkers, the Dolls' much-feared 90-millimeter cannons were very much in evidence. But suddenly, the uneven struggle became a victory for the defenders, when the bears' armored parachute platoon plummeted down in homemade parachutes from a birch tree on the edge of the woods.

The Wilderness

The town had originally been a trading post that was set up, shortly after the first expeditions had moved on, to trade with the trappers and with the inhabitants of distant and legendary places outside the grove. By now it had become a whole little community surrounded by a huddle of huts. The bears crowded into the main street together with a caravan just arrived from some distant country, its wagons loaded with expensive cloths and rare objects.

on the watch for bandits and desert villains, and other strays who occasionally criss-crossed the desolate landscape.

Hearth and Home

The rain pattered on the windowpanes in the teddy bears' house in Rabbit Street. It was gray and cold outside, and the weather was highly unsuitable for adventures. In the family room, Little Yellow and Elephant were discussing a chess problem that had been published in the latest issue of the *Teddy Bear Chronicle*. The fire in the open fireplace crackled and in came Rabbit with a tray of tea and cake. This was indeed a day on which to curl up by the fire at home in order to gather strength and plan new adventures.

The Desert

In a distant oasis, deep in the heart of the desert, flourished a small mining community. Its inhabitants were pioneers—adventurous bears who had dared to travel far from home and defy the dangers of the desert in order to extract valuable and mineral-rich ores out of deep shafts. The bears had suffered great hardships in their hideous struggle against hunger, thirst, and extremes of cold and heat, and had to be perpetually

Teddy Bear Fredriksson

Long ago when I was four
I had a present from my Dad,
I've kept that present ever since—
The finest gift I ever had.

Teddy Bear Fredriksson, yes, that was his name.
We loved each other—our life seemed a game.
Yes, Fredriksson was always there.
He was my best friend—that little bear.

His coat was furry, soft and thick.
He warmed me when we went to bed.
And once when I was very sick,
Teddy helped cure me, Father said.

Chorus: Teddy Bear Fredriksson, yes, that was his name . . .

But the years went by, and we grew apart.
I'm married, have a child, but my friend is sad.
So yesterday when my daughter was four,
She was given a teddy by her Dad.

Chorus: Teddy Bear Fredriksson . . .

"Teddy Bear Fredriksson" by Lars Berghagen. Illustrated by Vera Mulder.

Skipping Rhyme . . .

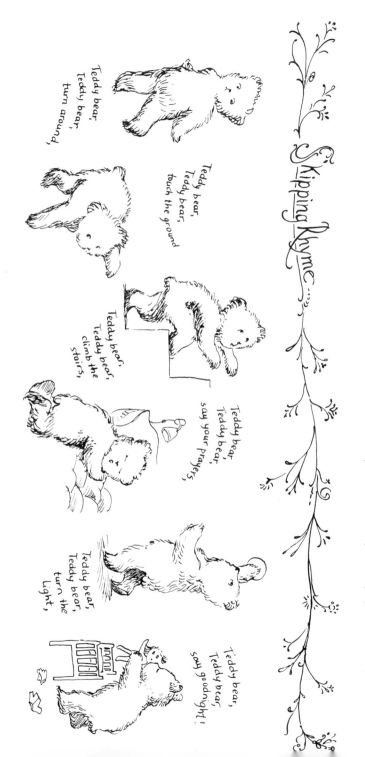

Teddy bear,
teddy bear,
turn around,

Teddy bear,
Teddy bear,
touch the ground

Teddy bear,
Teddy bear,
climb the
stairs,

Teddy bear,
Teddy bear,
say your prayers,

Teddy bear,
Teddy bear,
turn the
light,

Teddy bear,
Teddy bear,
say goodnight!

Little Teddy Bear

Oh, my poor little teddy bear,
Is your stomach rumbling?
How could I have left you there?
I just forgot you all day long!

Now you sit so sweet and kind
I suppose you're waiting for your food?
Come, open up, my bear—please mind,
And I'll give you something good.

Then one, two, three, to bed, that's it!
I'll tuck you in so nice and tight.
Until it's time to be up again,
You'll sleep quite soundly through the night.

From *Kleine beer* by Mia Bake; from
In Zwartjes Land, 1916.

105

Bear News

John and His Brothers

We are six small bears living in a basket. We used to go out with Mamma, one at a time, and then we were safely put in her pocket. When we had a birthday, we were given new clothes that Grandmother had crocheted.

Paul is a diver. He has become weighed down with always having to carry dive tanks on his back. Jonas is both the oldest and the largest. He has always been the oldest, but only the largest since he happened to get run over by Grandfather's car. Then he became almost twice as tall. Things always happened to Jonas, and as a result, he was kissed so much his nose turned quite shiny.

Ben is a rascal; some people even say he looks like a safecracker! Little Rosebud has a red jersey, and Mamma thinks he looks like a football player. Tony has been a seaman. My name is John, and everyone says I'm awfully nice.

106

Teddy Gustav Edgren

Gustav was born in Pörtö in Finland on August 23, 1937. As a child, he joined the Edgren family and was named after Field Marshal Gustav Mannerheim.

Gustav always went with Maria in her knapsack. On her way to school, they walked past army headquarters. One day they met Mannerheim himself, who was on his way to work. Maria opened the door for him and he then bowed politely and greeted both her and Gustav.

When war broke out in Finland in 1939, Maria sometimes had to run down to the shelter. Gustav was always calm then and protected her from the bombs. Maria was sent to Sweden as a child war refugee in 1943. Her brother went to another family, so Gustav had to be her brother instead.

Maria's mother had made all of Gustav's clothes. In 1940, he was given a dark suit, which is almost exactly like the one Maria's father had. The tailcoat was made in 1946 out of bits of cloth from a real old tailcoat, and the sailor costume was made in 1952. Gustav had also had a

Naturally, a passport is needed to travel abroad.

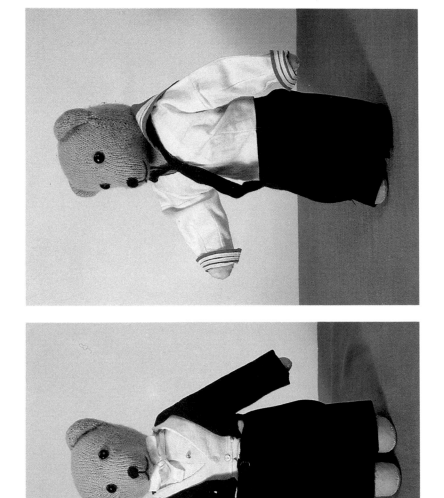

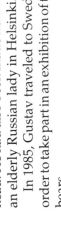

tropical suit, but the pants disappeared in Australia in 1970, when Maria and Gustav made a trip around the world. Gustav is particularly important on journeys, because he is the clear conscience that stops Maria from doing foolish things.

Gradually Gustav began to wear out and the sawdust started trickling out of him. Then Mother knitted him a new head. He had also been made new feet by an elderly Russian lady in Helsinki.

In 1985, Gustav traveled to Sweden in order to take part in an exhibition of teddy bears.

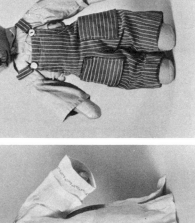

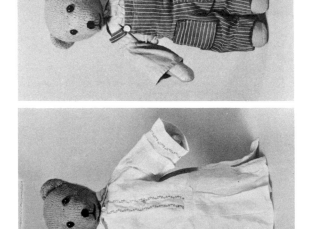

The Political Bear

The bear's role in political cartoons started long before the Teddy Roosevelt era and has since become even more important. When the leader of Sweden's People's Party, Bengt Westerberg, said that he liked teddy bears, he was at once presented with a large one. A photograph of him hugging his teddy bear appeared in the newspapers after his success in the 1985 election. Then, Westerberg in a foreign policy debate in 1986, painted the Soviet Union as the greatest threat to

world peace. The cartoonist seized upon the teddy bear to symbolize little Sweden kicking the huge Russian bear in the backside.

The bear as a symbol of Russia has ancient origins and has been used numerous times in caricatures and jokes. The varying fortunes of war in the Crimea from 1853 to 1856 can be followed in a series of "bear pictures" in the English humor magazine *Punch*. During that time, Turkey was at war with Russia and received aid from England, among other countries. The symbolism of the Russian bear varied: Sometimes it represented the Russian nation, sometimes the czar; sometimes bear cubs stood for the czar's sons. Turkey was usually portrayed as a

turkey. In the above cartoon from *Punch* in 1853, the Turks are portrayed as a swarm of bees attacking an annoyed Russian bear who caught with its paw on the beehive. The cartoon refers to the old story about the bear who tries to get at the honey in the beehive—even more relevant here, since the mosque in the background resembles a beehive.

The Danish newspaper Information reported in the summer of 1979 that the Bear Liberation Front (BLF) had occupied the town of Quistgard. It was never made clear whether this was true or not, but the BLF does appear at regular intervals here and there. Their political program is to fight against oppression in all forms and to create a society in which we care about each other.

From Topical in Politics, No. 5, 1977. Illustrated by Rune Andrén.

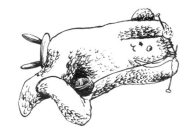

Homemade Bears

Children have always played with children's section of the popular homemade toys. The very first teddy bears, the ones we know so little about, were sure to have been made by some parent interested in bears, or by some adult friend. Rose Michtom's first teddy bear was made at home. So anyone who tries to make a teddy bear today is following an old tradition. Teddy bears are also often made today in kindergartens and in schools.

Patterns and inspiration to make a teddy bear can come from a great many directions. Only a few years after the birth of Teddy Bear, material with printed bear patterns was sold, ready to be cut out and sewn, and patterns for more complete teddy bears were offered by pattern firms.

Ladies World magazine and *Playthings* featured teddy bear patterns in 1907. An early pattern from Art Fabric Mills included the necessary buttons, pins and washers for making the joints, as well as shoe-buttons for the eyes.

In 1924, Butterick made a pattern for Deli-Bear, a little Teddy who had been featured as a cartoon character in the popular *Delineator* magazine. The other major pattern companies all have made, and still make, Teddy Bear patterns. The Vogue Bear made by Vogue Pattern Service, also

Björn Borg, made out of an old pair of long underwear, 1983. Design: Eva-Lena Bengtsson.

Teddy bear in black sheepskin made according to an ICA pattern in the 1940s.

Robertson, born in the 1920s, has been given a new coat of corduroy.

ICA mönster

features patterns for an extensive bear wardrobe. The Simplicity Pattern company made one for Paddington Bear.

There are many useful books on making one's own Teddy Bears, a few of which are listed in the bibliography.

Today, a great many directions for teddy bears that can be made at home—either sewn, knitted, or crocheted—are available. The patterns appear quite regularly in handicraft magazines and books, and are also sold individually. Some teddy bears are simple—perhaps just two pieces of material to be put together and stuffed—while others are more complicated, with a large number of pattern pieces. Most teddy bears purchased in stores are also made up of a large number of parts, perhaps offering a creatures with more individuality and character. But a teddy bear does not need to be perfect or intricately designed to be loved and accepted. Most important to the prospective owner seems to be how the teddy bear feels to the touch. A great many rejected teddy bears have had to hear that they were "too horrid to hold" or "felt too hard." Also important is the look in the teddy's eyes, which has to be right—and the teddy must be easy to make eye contact with. A real teddy bear should look us straight in the eye, with understanding and sympathy, as well as love.

Even quite small children can draw or make a simple teddy bear. In the process

of doing so, they develop a sense of belonging and confidence. The teddy bear that one creates oneself from start to finish is perhaps the most perfect bear, one that will be unique. But a teddy bear made with the help of someone else, even before it is finally born, creates warm ties between the people concerned. It reminds us of each other.

The Pattern

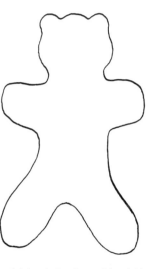

Anyone who wants to make a teddy bear can of course use a ready-made pattern. But that is not necessary. It is easy to draw a pattern yourself, and then with a few details make the bear into a personality. The advantage of making your own teddy bear pattern is that you get the teddy bear you want—short or tall, with short arms or long, and so on.

The simplest teddy bear pattern consists of two similar pieces. The bear is drawn from the front, with legs, arms, and ears connected to the body. The bear must be drawn wider than normal, because some of the width will be taken up by the stuffing. The neck should be wide enough to enable you to turn the sewn-up bear inside out and to make it easy to stuff the head. The teddy bear will also be easier to sew if it is drawn in soft curves instead of angles.

It is slightly more difficult to draw a pattern for a teddy bear in profile, but the body of a teddy of that kind has more character. Arms, legs, and ears are first sketched directly on the pattern for the body of the bear for positioning, but are then transferred to another piece of paper. Then all the parts are cut out separately. A little extra width will be needed for the arms and legs.

With stretch materials such as stretch terry cloth, velour, or cotton tricot, it is

112

sufficient to draw a bear in profile and cut out the parts in double-thickness material. In firmer materials, the bear will have a much better shape if it is complemented with an extra piece that stretches from nose to tail.

The Material

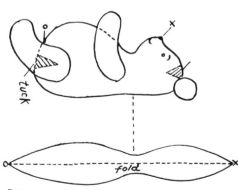

Design by Pernilla Mossberg and Birgit Landin.

A teddy bear should be made from material that has the right teddy bear feel in regard to pile and softness. Perhaps it is best to start by using some old material. An outgrown jersey, the fuzzy inside of a sweat shirt, a woolen lining, a plush bedspread, a college sweater, a velour or velveteen skirt, stretch corduroy pants—almost anything and everything can be used (except the worn parts!).

It's an advantage if the material stretches, since it is then easier to stuff the bear to the desired shape. Felt, which is not very durable, is best for small mascot bears or to make paws, footpads, and noses, or eyes.

For stuffing, cotton batting can be used, or kapok, carded wool, polyester fiber, and old nylon stockings or tricot strips. A worn-out quilt stuffed with synthetic padding can be made into a great many teddy bears. If the bear is for a very small

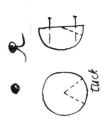

child, don't use plastic pieces, foam rubber, dried peas, or anything that can stick in your child's throat. For the same reason, avoid using glass or plastic eyes or bows, ribbons, or buttons for eyes, unless the teddy is for someone other than a small child. Embroidered eyes can be just as expressive.

Method

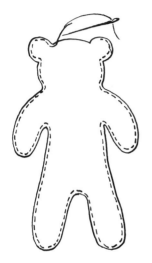

After you finish the pattern, place it on the material. On material with a pile, the pile must lie from top to bottom for all the bear parts; otherwise the color varies. On velvet materials, there will be a deeper luster if the pile is directed upward. The direction in which the material stretches is also important. The teddy bear will acquire the best shape if the material stretches along the breadth of the bear; then Teddy will have a nice round stomach.

Next, fold the material in half, with the pile facing inside, and pin on the teddy bear pattern. Trace around the pattern and then sew around the outline before cutting out the bear. That prevents the edges from curling up. Leave one side open for stuffing. After the bear is sewn, cut it out, leaving a 1/4-inch seam allowance; then turn it right side out.

With stretch materials, unless you use elastic thread, the normal machine stitch (or backstitch if sewn by hand) will not be satisfactory, so the bear should be sewn with either a zigzag or a buttonhole stitch. Thick pile material and felt are easily sewn together by hand, using a small backstitch. Smaller bears in a fur fabric can be stitched with the right side out. Felt bears can be sewn using a small running stitch on the right side of the material.

When filling the bear, make sure that the stuffing is evenly distributed throughout the entire body. Then sew up the opening with small backstitching. On simple bears, run two rows of basting around the neck; then pull the threads till the neck is the desired width. On bears for slightly older children, the neck can be pulled together with a ribbon.

Then all that's left is to add the details that make the teddy into a personality, from embroidering the eyes and nose to sewing on the arms, legs, and ears.

The Personality of a Teddy Bear

It is the minor details that make the personality of a teddy bear. Try moving the eyes on the pattern closer to each other or closer to the nose. The expression changes immediately. Put some thought into what it is that makes a bear a bear and not a cat. Is it the shape of the ears, the nose, or the proportions? Anyone who wants a bear-like teddy bear would be wise to study real bears to see what they look like.

Nose. The nose is a protruding detail.

113

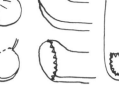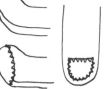

The simplest method is just to embroider a small round dot, or to add a nose and mouth, as shown.

A protruding nose can be made of a circle with a tuck sewn into it. The nose is then pinned to the face and sewn on before the various parts of the bear are sewn together. Turn the material to the wrong side and carefully cut a slit where the nose will be located. Then stuff the nose and sew up the slit.

Sometimes it is easier to sew on the finished nose by hand when the bear is complete. Then the stuffing is pushed in from the front, after which only a small seam remains to be stitched closed. The nose and mouth can be embroidered together with the eyes after the bear has been sewn together and stuffed.

Paw Pads. These can be sewn to the paws, using a zigzag stitch, before the front and back are sewn together.

Leather pads can be sewn by hand to the bottom of the feet, after the legs have been sewn and stuffed. The foot then acquires volume.

Ears. The shape and position of the ears

also influence the bear's personality. If the ears are to be sewn to the head, you can try making tucks or wrinkling the ears at the bottom. A little stuffing in the ears gives them volume and firmness. On teddy bears whose ears and head have been cut from one piece, a seam sewn after stuffing can accentuate the beginning of the ear.

Clothes and Equipment

The personality of the teddy bear is further emphasized by clothes, which humanize the bear and give it a profession, hobby, sex, social status, or age. Whatever anyone says or feels about bears wearing clothes, a bear walking in the mountains must at least have a knapsack on his back, must he not?

Fluffy small bears. Design by Gunilla Sjöberg.

114

Winnie-the-Pooh made from a pattern in profile. Design by Cecilia Hagström.

A More Difficult Bear to Make

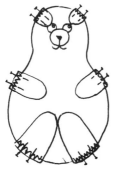

body
2 ea

Material: Sturdy material for larger bears (plush, velour, corduroy, pile, fake fur); thread; ribbon.

Seams: For stretch materials, use a zigzag stitch or elastic thread.

Procedure: Draw your own teddy bear pattern. Cut out all parts, leaving a 1/4-inch seam allowance.

Sew up the "angle" of the nose. Zigzag stitch the nose onto the face on the right side. Cut an X in the material at the back of the nose and stuff the nose.

Sew all around except leave a side opening. Turn right side out.

Stuff the head and body of the bear. Sew up the opening by hand.

Tie a ribbon around the neck.

nose

Zigzag on (or embroider) the eyes and mouth.

Sew up the ears on the inner side. Trim the seam and turn the ears right side out.

ear 4 ea.

Using a zigzag stitch, attach the paw pads on the arms and legs. Sew one side of the arms and legs in the same way as the ears. Stuff the arms and legs.

arms cut 3 of each

Pin on the ears, arms, and legs so that they lie in toward the body (paw pads toward the stomach). Pin the back of the body on top, right side to right side. Cross-pin, or the layers of cloth will slide.

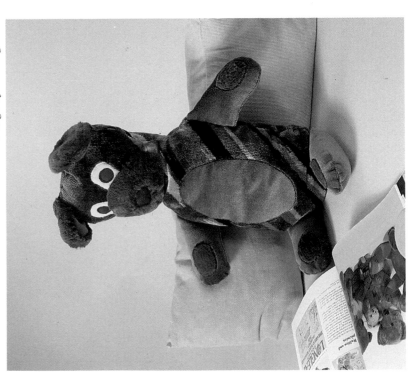

Design by Eva Engman.

115

Other Kinds of Bear Sewing

A teddy bear can be much more than an ordinary teddy bear. He can be made into a glove or finger puppet, a pajama case, a cushion, a bag, a rug, an appliqué for clothes, or a brooch. Try adding bear ears to a favorite cap. And laying your head on a teddy bear cushion and wrapping yourself up in a teddy bear blanket are not bad ideas, are they?

Bears made at Textile Teacher Training, Uppsala, 2d Year, 1984. Treatment and pattern by Birgit Landin and Gunilla Sjöberg.

116

Knitted or Crocheted Teddy Bears

Teddy can also be a pattern on a sweater.

Bears can also be knitted or crocheted. Draw a pattern first; then knit or crochet a trial piece and count the number of stitches per inch. Then follow the pattern. It is simplest to knit or crochet the bear in two straight pieces, which are then sewn together. After the bear is stuffed, stitch along the ears at the top, embroider the nose and eyes and draw a running thread round the neck. Body, head, and limbs can also be knitted or crocheted, stuffed separately, then sewn together.

Detailed directions for knitting or crocheting teddy bears can also be found in handicraft magazines or books.

Teddy bear face to crochet. This can then be sewn onto a sweater, bag, or jacket. Two faces sewn together become a purse for a small child.

Scout Teddy Bear

My life began some time in the 1970s when I was given to Ann-Marie as a Christmas present. She wasn't all that interested in me at first. Life was dull until the day her older brother took me with him to scout camp. Then I discovered what fun it was to be in the great outdoors.

In 1980, I was given a scout uniform of shirt, pants, and scarf. Ann-Marie gradually fell for my extraordinary charm, and when she became a girl scout, she and her brother took turns in taking me with them into the woods. Ann-Marie has also made me a knapsack, and in it is most of what you need—stove, canteen, bandaids, and so on. You also have to keep a lookout at night for grizzly bears and other horrors, but you can fall asleep occasionally. Ann-Marie's mother made my sleeping bag, which is really nice and warm.

I don't want to boast, but I soon became the teddy bear mascot of the entire scout troop. No hikes without me!

A little bear.

The Bear in Comic Strips

Comic strips began to become popular at the turn of the century, and as early as that, the bear could be found in them. Since then, numerous bears and teddy bears have wandered through these cartoon strips. Personalities like Yogi Bear, Rasmus Bear and Teddy Bear from Saga Land (from two Danish series), Baloo (from Rudyard Kipling's *Jungle Book*), and Bamse (from a Swedish comic strip) have acquired friends of all ages. Week after week, they share with us a piece of themselves and their lives—thus becoming part of ourselves and our lives.

The small bears pull Santa Claus's sleigh.

From Emblem to Cartoon

The first comic strip bear is a few years older than the teddy, and the same age as the cartoon series in general. In 1892, the *San Francisco Examiner* published drawings of actual events, done by James Swinnerton. The main characters were some little bears, and their prototypes were, in fact, the small bears in the emblem on the state flag of California. The drawings, called *Little Bears*, developed into a series. Later on, they were called *Little Bears and Tykes* and *Little Bears and Tigers*, according to the characters in them.

Richard Outcault's *The Yellow Kid* and other early cartoon series were satirical and entertaining. In *Little Bears*, Swinnerton had brought a symbol of power—the bear—down to a comic level. During the first great teddy bear

Animals, Comic Strips, Cartoon Films, and People

When animals became characters in comic strips, centuries of tradition and symbolic values had already characterized them. The cat was independent, the dog faithful, and the fox cunning. Ever since the ancient fables, humanized animals, with the characteristics and foibles of real people, have been a popular theme. The arrival of the comic strip series offered an even better medium, in which a spark of life

popularity wave in the United States, the earliest cartoon series about teddy bears was credited: *Little Johnny and the Teddy Bears*. This was drawn by John Rudolph Bray and first published in 1907 in the American magazine *Judge*.

situations. All of us, and children in particular, have a need to recognize ourselves in others so that our feelings can be confirmed and accepted. Take, for instance, Bamse, who is strong but most of all helpful, or his friend Little Hop, a small, frightened rabbit who always overcomes his fears. From reading about Bamse and Hop children learn that it is permissible to be both powerful and good, scared yet brave. Since bears are usually portrayed as good-natured yet bumbling creatures, they particularly attract children, who often see their own good intentions misunderstood.

Bear or teddy bear?

It is sometimes difficult to decide whether a drawing is of a teddy bear or a "real" bear. The teddy bear, however, has certain distinctive features you can't miss. You can see that it has jointed arms and legs, exposed seams, and patches on the paws. The coat is generally less hairy than on ordinary bears, the eyes are larger and rounder, and the stance is straighter. Ordinary bears usually have a little tail, which a teddy bear never has.

American Comic Strip Bears

Although Walt Disney is most famous for Donald Duck and Mickey Mouse, he, or rather Walt Disney Productions, also has created several well-known bear

The comic strip Muff and Tuff by K. Frykstrand.

could be blown into the mute, and beloved or frightening, animals. Who has not put a scarf around the family dog's neck or had long conversations with a cat, doll, or teddy bear? In the world of comic strips, our fantasies and fancies become visible. For instance, it is regarded as natural for the dog Snoopy to wear a cap and scarf as it is for any other character in the series to do so, and that the Swedish Bamse actually speaks is as obvious as the fact that he exists. If a picture says more than a thousand words, just imagine what a series of pictures with words can say!

In our society, both children and animals are dependent on others and they find it difficult to change their conditions. In literature, children and animals are often portrayed as akin to each other; for instance, only innocent children are able to understand animals and can even handle wild animals.

In animal series, it is easy for children to identify themselves with the characters and imagine themselves in various

1. Tuff: "The best hair tonic, that'd be something for us! Look what healthy-looking hair Uncle Felix has since he started using it."

2. Muff: "It was awfully expensive, Tuff. But it'll be fun to have lovely long hair, and just think how pleased Mom will be. She always has so much trouble brushing us and getting our hair to grow."

3. Tuff: "Let's help each other. Sit still about it! But oh, what the teddy bea... I'll pour the hair tonic onto your back, but I'll leave half the bottle, then you can rub it into me."

4. The hair tonic was so good, no dou... looked like when they woke the ne... morning. And they'd thought Mo... would be pleased!

BRUM IS THE HOME OF A LITTLE BEAR WHO LIVES IN THE FOREST...

Brum meets the world in his first comic strip picture.

Teddy, from Tuff and Tuss, 1954.

characters. As early as 1924, Disney produced a short film version of *Goldilocks and the Three Bears* called *Alice and the Three Bears*. Bears such as Winnie-the-Pooh, Bruno Bear, Brother Bear, Bongo, Baloo, and Little John all first appeared in Disney film cartoons before becoming comic strip characters.

Winnie-the-Pooh largely follows its literary model and its illustrations by Ernest H. Shepard. Bruno Bear is a clothed bear with limited intelligence—that is what gives the series its amusing points. Brother Bear lives together with, among others, Brother Fox and Brother Rabbit in Disneyland's large forest. He, like Pooh and Bruno Bear, is not noted for his ability to think, and so is exploited, as in the fables, often by Brother Fox, or is cheated by Brother Rabbit. Bongo, on the other hand, is smarter and gets himself out of all traps. He is a runaway circus bear, who meets a pretty girl bear in the forest, but also encounters a villainous bear, who is more uncivilized. The latter has no clothes, for instance, and acts nasty and looks unkempt.

Baloo from Rudyard Kipling's *Jungle Book* and Little John from the English

legend of Robin Hood are large bears, naive and full of self-confidence, but dependent on others—Bagheera the panther and Robin the fox—to achieve anything. Mowgli, the human child, likes being with animals and living in the jungle, and Baloo the bear wins the boy's heart. But the end is inevitable and traditional. Mowgli must return to civilization and people, and leaves the life of the jungle (childhood) for a girl.

When William Hanna and Joe Barbara left Disney for a career of their own, they took with them a figure of a bear in a

In *Bamse*, No. 72, 1984, Rune Andrésson tells of his forty years as an illustrator of comic strips. In cartoon form, he shows what happened when Teddy Bear drew and talked on television. Teddy is at the drawing board and Rune himself is behind the camera.

The Sandpit, by Joakim Pirinen, April 1986.

national park who became the main character in the comic strip series called *Yogi Bear*. Yogi's passion in life is food, which he constantly begs off visitors to the

European Bears

A bear does not always have to be the main character to have a dominating position in a cartoon series. In the Dutch *Tom Puss*, by Martin Toonder, Tom Puss is a little white cat. His best friend, and the reader's friend, is a bear, the wealthy gentleman Oliver B. Bumble of the Bumblestone Castle estate. Bumble is a kindly, friendly, and very naive bear. He likes the good life, and he keeps his gentlemanly dignity. In his unsuspecting innocence, Bumble is easily exploited by rogues, or ends in difficult situations. Then Tom Puss steps in and helps his friend.

Winnie-the-Pooh and his friends ponder over Eeyore's wish to be famous. From Winnie-the-Pooh, No. 11, 1984. © 1987 Walt Disney Company

Yogi Bear

park. He's kind but stupid, and is always creating trouble for park wardens. Fortunately, Yogi has a friend, a cleverer and more level-headed bear, who supervises Yogi's activities as best he can.

With the advent of television in the average home, many animators turned to the new medium. *Yogi* started as a television series in the 1950s. Its success led to the publication of comic strips and books.

The relationship between Tom Puss and Bumble has a parallel in the Belgian series *Tintin*, in which Captain Haddock plays the part of Bumble. (The captain is also an old sea bear!) In both series, Bumble and Captain Haddock represent the comical effects and what is to come. Tom Puss and Tintin are inventive and quick-thinking, but quite pale and insignificant characters. They function as starting points for the series and for the gallery of personalities that collects around them.

Superman, it is a teddy bear who, with his ability to fly and his supernatural powers, is at the service of mankind. With a swift movement, he whips off his bear coat, exposing his red Superman costume.

Teddy Bear in his fur coat has become as ordinary as Clark Kent in his everyday suit. In order to achieve something, SuperTed has to creep out of his skin. This reminds us that we never know what lies hidden behind what we see. Could the wild bear be a prince in disguise, or the teddy bear a superman?

Another of Martin Toonder's series has a panda as its main character. Toonder's "cat-bear" Panda resembles in character and appearance both Tom Puss the cat and Bumble the bear.

The "superman" tradition of comic strips has had a direct impact on the bears. It started with a television series called *SuperTed*, drawn by the Englishman, Mike Young. This has since been published in booklets. Both form and action in *SuperTed* are a paraphrase of comic strips with superheroes. Instead of

…nald Duck, No. 2, 1949.
…87 Walt Disney Company

Rupert Bear

Rupert Bear is one of England's most popular comic strips and has been translated into approximately eighteen languages. The series has run almost daily in the *Daily Express* since November, 1920.

The strip began with Little Lost Bear, who was drawn by Mary Tourtel. She drew the series until 1935, when she was forced to stop because of poor eyesight. It was taken over by Alfred Bestall, who worked on it for forty years. Then it was drawn by Jim Henderson and, most recently, by John Harrold.

Rupert is a boy teddy bear who lives with his parents in the small English town of Nutwood. He is a bright, inquisitive, good-natured bear. If he comes up against problems or injustices, he has to intervene. Every new episode begins as he leaves home in the morning on an outing or an errand, but he always returns. Leaving home and returning is a common theme in children's books, because it symbolizes the natural process by which children free themselves from their parents.

Physically, Rupert looks like an ordinary boy. He is fully clothed, has hands with fingers, and wears shoes on his feet. The only thing that reminds you he is a bear is his head. Mary Tourtel's original drawing indicated a seam in his head, which made him into a teddy bear. His appearance has since changed, and today it is more difficult to decide whether he is a teddy bear or a bear.

So the Bear family are bears or teddy bears, while the other inhabitants of Nutwood are different kinds of animals, but also human. Clothed animals and people speak the same language and mix with each other without friction. Rupert is also bilingual and can talk to ordinary

animals in a special animal language. In one episode, Rupert is captured by a circus and shut in with circus animals. They urge him to flee; otherwise he will become like them, that is, an ordinary animal who can't talk to humans. Rupert manages to escape and is allowed to keep his boy identity.

In earlier episodes, in the 1920s, supernatural creatures such as witches,

Oliver B. Bumble becomes a bridegroom, Dagens Nyheter, January 25, 1986.

elves, magicians, and wind gods were often introduced. The series was strongly linked with older fairy tales and books such as *Alice in Wonderland*. At that time, Rupert was also much more of a teddy

Panda and Kalkomobile, 1984.

Primary School Children's Newspaper in the 1930s and 1940s, and was created by Kerstin Frykstrand. Muff and Tuff were two nice bears, who played marvelous games and got involved in small misadventures, which ended happily. They often caused Mother Bear trouble, but she always forgave them.

In 1944, another Swedish bear opened his bright brown eyes—Brum, drawn by Rune Andréasson. Brum was a little bear cub and the main character in the Allers magazine series *Adventures among Animals*, 1944 – 67.

In 1950, Andréasson started a new comic strip called *Teddy's Adventures*. In contrast to Brum, Teddy wore clothes and was tremendously strong. He was also rather dull.

In the 1950s, Andréasson expanded the fauna of Swedish comic strip bears with yet another in *Teddy Bear Draws and Tells Stories*. This series began as television programs introduced by a real trick-

SuperTed at the Amusement Park, 1986. Illustrators: Rob Lee and Ian Henderson.

bear, or toy bear, who in a "more natural" way was able to move between these two worlds. When Alfred Bestall took over, much of the fairy tale character disappeared and the series became more realistic, with Rupert more like a boy.

Rupert's great popularity has extended far beyond just readers of the series, and as early as the 1920s, a fan club was started in England, the Rupert League. The series, already in books and animated television features, has given rise to various Rupert objects for children, such as mugs, clothes, and toys.

Muff and Tuff

Muff and Tuff was the first Swedish cartoon series with teddy bears as the main characters. It was published in the

Rupert and His Pet Monkey, by Mary Tourtel, Daily Express, 1933.

Rupert is drawn today by John Harrold. Although people and places are done more schematically than before, they are still "old-fashionedly" realistic. From Rupert and Alaric Flee, 1986.

filmed teddy bear sitting at a drawing board and presenting drawn or told stories. Later, it became a comic strip series in weekly papers.

In the 1950s, there was much public discussion about the damage that could be done to children devouring so many comics. One of those children was Joakim Pirinen, who, in 1983, published *Welcome to the Sand Pit*, a book of short episodes with a sand pit as background. In them, Pirinen has children appear in other forms, among them the teddy bear. The sand pit, similar to a wildlife reserve, is a sanctuary, but one that has been allocated to children. In portraying the children as teddy bears, the author reveals their vulnerability, as well as their dignity.

Another Swedish comic strip series is *Bobo*, which is published as a magazine for small children. Created by Göran F. Ek and Lasse Mortimer, Bobo is a troll bear. (A troll in Scandinavian legend is a dwarf or giant who lives in caves or hills.) This Smurf-like creature originally lived in Boboland, but now lives in the Bo Cave in Seven Mile Woods, Bo Cave is the center of everything that happens in the great forest. Bobo is a friendly soul who helps everyone, especially his best friend Lisa, the doll. To help him—and to get the intrigue going—Bobo has a lucky telescope. It can move him to the place he sees in the telescope and can be used only by a bobo.

Bamse

Bamse, by Rune Andréasson, is one of the most popular comic strip characters in Sweden. Born in *Allers Family Magazine* in 1966, he became a television star the same year. Andréasson gave up the series in *Allers* in order to publish his own magazine, and in 1973, the comic strip magazine *Bamse* came out. At the same time, seven new Bamse films started to be shown on television, followed by two more in 1981.

Bamse is yet another example of how different media support one another. The popular Bamse is also found printed on tee shirts, games, puzzles, savings banks, and many other objects. In 1980, Bamse appeared on a stamp, and since 1985, the Free Theatre has shown the musical called *Bamse*.

Bamse Bear lives in a community with other humanized animals. The environment is forest and mountain country, but sometimes Bamse may travel to a nearby town. He is small, but becomes the "strongest bear in the world" when he eats his grandmother's thunder-honey. With his enormous strength, he manages to get himself and others out of all kinds of difficulties. Bamse's friends are Hop

(Skutt), the scared little rabbit, and the sleepy but shrewd Shellman (Skalman), who can carry the bulkiest of objects. If Bamse's strength is not sufficient, Shellman can always fish out another invention from his shell. The original mother and source of all strength in the series is Bamse's paternal grandmother, with her thunder-honey made from a secret recipe. From her elevated place on the High Mountain through her telescope she can keep an eye on everything that happens.

In 1981, Bamse married the pretty Brummelisa, with whom he has since had five cubs. Since then, the series has portrayed a great deal of what it is like to live with a family of children. The way the Bamse family solve their problems can be an answer to the reader's own questions.

Teddy Bear from Saga Land

Teddy Bear from Saga Land (Teddy and Lisa) is a Danish comic strip series from the mid-1930s. It was written by Elisabet

Rasmus Bear and Kalle Tuff, 1975.

The teddy on this Italian diaper pack reveals the diapers Rasmus perhaps hides.

Greeve and drawn by Harry Nielsen. At the end of the 1970s, the series was taken over by Ulrich Jensen and George Humble.

Teddy is a teddy bear, who, together with his friend Lisa the doll, has various adventures. Just like Rupert, Teddy is inquisitive, inventive, and good-natured. In his relationship to Lisa, he is the one who acts and takes the initiative. Lisa is more passive, though she is just as bright. Theirs is an affectionate relationship. They constantly exchange appreciative smiles and remarks. Their relationship could be compared with one between an older brother and younger sister.

When Teddy and Lisa are not having adventures, they live in the nursery of a girl called Greta. From there, all journeys start—to Sleeping Beauty, Princess Spring, Toyland, or wherever. A child's (Greta's) relationship to her teddy bear is portrayed in the series.

Rasmus Bear

Another popular bear comic strip series stems from Denmark, *Rasmus Bear* (*Rasmus Klump*) by Vilhelm and Carla Hansen. It started in 1951 and has run as a daily strip in seventy-five newspapers in eight countries. Altogether, some twenty-nine episodes have been published as albums and been translated into twelve languages.

The Rasmus Teddy series contains only animals, all of whom are just as humanized as Rasmus. In the first section, Rasmus and his friends built the boat called *Mary*, which for a while carried the friends on their adventures. Rasmus's friends are Sealy the seal, Pingo the Penguin, and Pelle the pelican. In the group, it is Rasmus who is in command. He takes the initiative and is the obvious leader. Sealy is an ex-sailor, a leisurely person who seldom takes his hands out of

little brother, Pelle the big sister, and Sealy the grandfather.

Torty the tortoise and Froggie the Frog,

Bamse savings banks. The honey jar is where the treasure is hidden.

his pockets. Pingo is Rasmus's right-hand man and is mostly a step behind him. Pelle always has a solution handy and corrects Rasmus when he does anything wrong. Pelle the Pelican that he is, he has a large beak from which he can extract whatever is needed to cope with critical situations. Just like Harpo Marx, Mary Poppins, and Shellman (from the story of Bamse), he can come up with the most incredible objects. If, for instance, Rasmus needs a saw in the middle of the forest, Pelle just opens his beak—and there it is. The whole group is like a family, though without parents. Rasmus is the child, Pingo the

who are called "the little ones," also belong to the group. They play on their own in the background, too small to take

This picture clearly shows Bamse's double genetic heritage. Nose, ears, and tail show he is related to the polar bear on which he rides, while his cap, strength, and movements place him in the world of gnomes and other mysterious creatures. "Bamse's Busy Christmas." From Bamse, No. 2, 1983.

First day at kindergarten. Bamse, No. 10, 1984.

129

part in adventures. Their presence emphasizes the feeling of delight in discovery that is presented in the series. Just as Rasmus is delighted by new discoveries, the reader is delighted to discover the "little ones."

The Living Teddy Bear

Rupert Bear and Teddy Bear from Saga Land are teddy bears who live partly in the land of fairy tales and partly in the real world. Rupert mixes just as naturally with supernatural creatures, living toys in a comic strip world where the difference between fantasy and realism is only geographical. In *Rupert Bear*, the mixture of saga and reality is obvious, while in *Teddy Bear from Saga Land*, it is emphatically a child's view of reality that is being shown.

Teddy and Lisa live with Greta, who is in the seven-to-eleven age group. The

Although the dishwashing tub and the stove look old-fashioned, Bamse is a modern bear who takes his cap off in the house and washes up after meals. The Big News, Bamse No. 8, 1981.

adventures Teddy and Lisa experience all start when Greta reads from a book of fairy tales and begins to fantasize or dream. Teddy and Lisa then enter Greta's fantasy worlds.

There is yet another dimension that is linked with the special ability of the comic strip to merge reality with fantasy. Greta does not regard Teddy and Lisa simply as toys; she also views them as living creatures. And the worlds of her imagination are similarly not just fantasy but also reality. It is true that Greta knows what the physical reality looks like, but what is important is that she allows herself this game with her thoughts and that it can be included in her perception of reality. Greta gives Teddy and Lisa life—that is, she regards them as alive. In the series, the reader participates in Greta's way of understanding reality.

In the "realistic" parts of the series—in which Greta and other people take part—Teddy and Lisa sit rigidly still. Here, they are drawn as toys—in other words, inanimate objects. That Greta nevertheless regards them as alive is shown by the fact that they move their eyes a little and that in the text they talk to each other. When Teddy and Lisa are left alone in the pictures, and the fantasy world enters, they at once become mobile and fully alive. That they then take over the action is also shown in the way they grow in relation to the size of the picture.

A Good-Natured Creature

In bear and teddy bear cartoon series, the bear is usually the child's friend or alter ego. Bears can be divided into two main types, according to their qualities. One type is slow-thinking and lazy, like Baloo and Yogi; the other is enterprising and

NALLE från Sagolandet

Nu är det vår igen, och Nalle och Lisa har kommit tillbaka till lilla Greta.

1. »Det regnar så rysligt», sade Greta. »Jag kan varken arbeta i trädgården eller gå ut och gå med Nalle och Lisa. Vad skall jag göra, mamma?»

2. Men efter en stund hade Greta hittat på att hon skulle städa i sitt leksaksskåp. Och där bland alla leksakerna hittade hon en gammal sagobok.

3. När Greta hade städat färdig i skåpet kröp hon upp i soffan tillsammans med Nalle och Lisa och började läsa högt för dem ur den spännande sagoboken.

4. Det var en väldigt rolig saga, så alla tre blev förfärligt besvikna när de fann att slutet var borta. Någon hade ryckt loss de sista bladen.

5. »Jag måste ha tag i de där sidorna som fattas», sade Greta och började rota i skåpet igen. »Annars får vi ju inte veta hur det går».

6. »Ja, tänk om vi inte får veta hur det går», sade Lisa till Nalle. Men just när hon sade det blev prinsen i sagan livslevande och kom utridande ur sagoboken.

7. Det var faktiskt trolleri, men Nalle och Lisa blev inte alls rädda. De tyckte bara att det var roligt att se den ståtlige prinsen som Greta just hade läst om.

8. »Nu skall ni få uppleva slutet på sagan», sade prinsen. — »Men får inte Greta vara med?» undrade Lisa. — »Jo visst», sade prinsen, »men hon måste somna först».

9. Så snart Greta hade somnat stod sagoprinsen och Nalle och Lisa på hennes säng och ropade på henne. Och hon reste sig genast upp igen.

10. Alla tre satte sig upp på prinsens vita häst. Nalle satt sist, och han fick hålla sig väl i Lisa för att inte falla av. Och så bar det i väg.

11. De red rakt in i sagoboken, och så sade prinsen: »Blunda nu och önska er till Sagolandet. Om ni önskar riktigt ivrigt, så kommer vi dit».

12. Mycket riktigt! När de åter öppnade ögonen befann de sig i Sagolandet. De var på en landsväg, och rakt emot dem kom en katt som jamade så ynkligt.

Vad vill katten, tror du? Ja, det får du se nästa gång.

N:r 18

37

The transition from reality to dream world in Teddy Bear from Saga Land is shown in the accompanying drawings. The first picture is a scene in the real world. Teddy and Lisa are toys sitting quite still and mute. And yet, as the scenes progress, we can see that Greta doesn't regard the toys as soulless, because she is reading a story to them. Although the end of the story is missing, suddenly the prince steps out of the story book. Teddy and Lisa then come alive, but for Greta to be able to join in on the adventure, she first has to go to sleep. Then Teddy, Lisa, and the prince all call her. Gradually, as their relationships adjust, the prince becomes a fully grown man, while Greta, Teddy, and Lisa are all the size of children. Not 'til then does the real adventure story start.

adventurous, like Rasmus Bear and Teddy Bear from Saga Land.

The first type is fairly passive, but nevertheless quite a lot happens to these bears because of their innocent, naive, and indiscriminating relationship with the world around them. A bear like this often loves food and is a jovial person who enjoys life.

The other type is active and becomes involved in adventures because of his inquisitive and playful search for excitement. Common to both types is their good nature. It is the good bear taking shape before our eyes, a sympathetic soul who asserts himself against injustices and opponents. For the most part, the dangerous bear—the bear who is a threat—has gone from the world of comics. The bear's great strength remains, but it is used on the side of good.

Two bears, one small and the other large, often appear in the same series. By relating the little bear to the larger bear, a frame of reference is created for size and what that can characterize. A child reading the series is at the same time also provided with a "double" identification.

The bear is round in shape, his center of gravity low in his body, a defensive center that can also be found in other series characters. An aggressive center of gravity is high, prepared to attack. Aggressive attributes such as fangs and claws are absent in most comic strip series bears. An exception is Baloo, but then he lives in the jungle and has to be prepared to defend himself and Mowgli against Shere Khan the tiger.

The child reader soon finds out that the bear in a series is at the service of the child and pleads the child's case with adults. Who wouldn't want a friend like that?

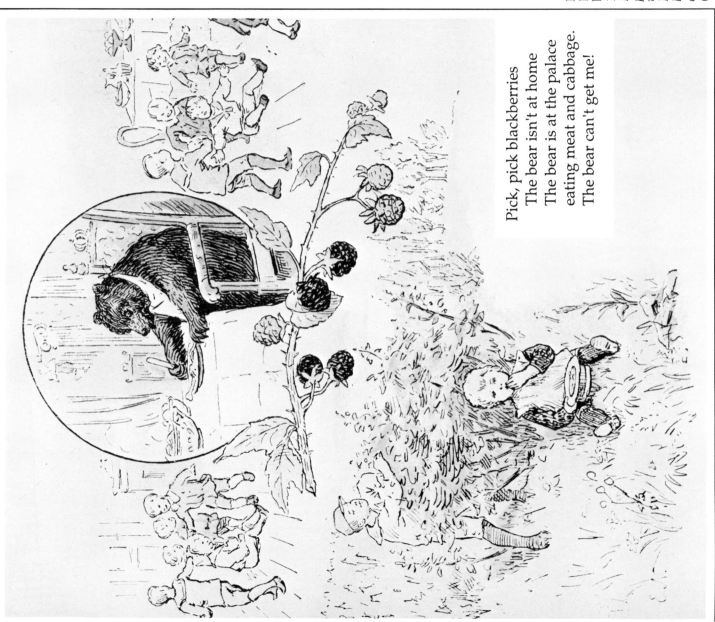

Pick, pick blackberries
The bear isn't at home
The bear is at the palace
eating meat and cabbage.
The bear can't get me!

Norwegian Picture Book for Children by Elling Holst, 1888. Illustrated by Eivind Nielsen. The poem uses a play on words: In Norwegian, blackberries are called bjornebaer (bearberries).

Bear Lore

In countries where bears were plentiful, especially Northern Europe, Asia, and North America, there are a great many references to bears in the native folklore. Many of the legends sought to provide an explanation for what was unknown in the life of the bear; others told of various ways of protecting yourself against bears. In some countries the bear is associated with magic and cult practices. Even today, the Japanese Ainu people still celebrate an annual fall festival at which they ritually kill and consume a bear cub that has been raised by them. Many of the songs and dances about bears are perhaps quite simply the remnants of other old bear cults. With ancestors of that kind, the teddy bear really is a magical animal!

Respect and Strength

According to Swedish folklore, the bear has "the strength of twelve men and the sense of one." But the bear's strength was desirable. It was believed that anyone who drank blood or gall from a newly killed bear could himself receive some of the bear's strength. It was also said to be just as effective to lace one's liquor with bear gall. On top of that, whoever drank the liquor also became fit and healthy! (At least, if you believe what was said in the far north of Sweden.)

Many examples of how the "forest grandfathers," as the bear is sometimes called, are respected and feared can be found in the nineteenth century. To calm and flatter the bear, it was common to assign it descriptive names. Some were friendly like Honey Paw, while others said something about the bear's ferocity.

The Bear as Werewolf

The most dangerous guise attributed to a bear is that of a werewolf. That alone is a measure of how important the bear was in older folklore. The most usual form of the werewolf was that of a wolf, but in northern Sweden, the werewolf sometimes acquired bear names.

According to legend, any individual who wanted to be a werewolf used a troll ring or a belt threaded over his body. To become human again, one must crawl through the belt again, but backwards. If someone else was behind the spell, it was harder to break. You then had to be addressed by your correct name, or else someone had to give the werewolf a meal. These legends are reminiscent of the sagas about the monster and the girl in which the girl's goodness enables the prince to rise out of his bear guise.

How to Protect Yourself

A great many legends describe how to protect yourself from the bear. Some methods may really have worked; others depended mostly on faith.

To keep the bear away from cornfields, farmers lit a fire, something the bears hated. According to another story, a girl caught out alone in the field in the summer could frighten a bear away by crying: "Shoot, men, the bear is here!" At the same time, the girl would thrash around with a strong branch, making a lot of noise, so that the bear would think there were armed men around and lope off.

Especially for a woman, it was not easy to stand eye to eye with a bear. A common legend concerns a lone woman who meets a bear in the forest. She undresses and exposes herself to the bear, who, embarrassed by the situation, turns away. Sometimes the bear is so embarrassed that it puts its paws over its eyes and leaves.

The Bear and Hibernation

The bear's long winter sleep, similar to a state of hibernation, has given rise to many speculations. Why does it hibernate? What does it do there? How does it know when it is time to hibernate and when it is time to come out?

In some northern European countries, it is said that when the bear is on its way to hibernate, it is careful that no one follows it. So before it goes into its sleeping place, the bear lies hidden on a bed of spruce branches for two weeks. There it waits and listens to find out if anything is coming after it, then goes calmly into the den.

How does the bear survive during that long sleep? Some old tales say that an old troll woman comes with blood for the bear; others say that it sucks its paws or stops up its anal sphincter.

When half the winter has gone, the bear turns over. In Sweden, this happens on *bear-turning day*, sometime between the end of January and the end of February, depending on the part of the country. When the bear turns, it is easily disturbed, so no noisy work can be done on bear-turning day. If the bear is disturbed, it may take revenge later on by clawing domestic animals.

When spring comes, the bear leaves its den. As it is hungry, it goes at once to an anthill. And then, it is said, the bear has only to stick out its tongue, and the ants crawl down its throat.

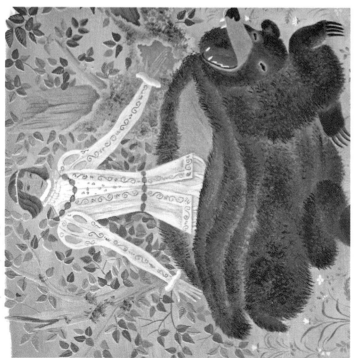

From Gullet and Rosebud *by Erna and Gösta Knutsson, 1956. Illustrated by Gustaf Tenggren.*

American Indian Lore

Some Indian tribes, such as the Apache, considered bears so sacred that they not only refused to kill them, but deemed them untouchable, alive or dead. Other Indians killed bears for food, but always apologized to the animal and treated the hide and bones with reverence.

Many Indian tribes, such as the Zuni, the Iroquois, and the Cree, perform bear dances, usually for medicinal purposes. The shamen (priests, or medicine men) dance in complete bearskins or masks and take on the curative powers of the bear. The Chippewa are said to "follow the bear path." That is, they use the wonderful medicines revealed to them by the bear. Among the Plains tribes, the bear dance has become a huge annual social celebration.

The Bear and the Pregnant Woman

According to legend, the bear can see if a woman is pregnant. He can also tell whether she is expecting a boy or a girl. If it's a boy, the bear is angry and seizes her. If it's a girl, he leaves her alone.

Once a pregnant Lapp woman happened to meet a bear. The bear was going to take her, because he could see she was carrying a boy child. As the woman ran away, she pulled off her dress and put it on a tree stump with her cap on top. When the bear came running and caught sight of the stump, he thought is was the woman. He ran over and clawed and tugged at the stump. Meanwhile the woman managed to get away.

Backword

Winnie-the-Pooh is a bear with a very small brain. He doesn't try to be clever like Owl, nor does he grumble about life like Eeyore. Pooh takes things as they come. Whatever happens, he maintains his philosophical calm and finds something to be pleased about.

"Well, what do you think, Pooh?" I said.
"Think about what?" asked Pooh.
"The Tao of Pooh, of course."
"The *how* of Pooh?" asked Pooh.
"Do we have to go through *that* again?" I said.
"Go through *what* again?" asked Pooh.
"The Tao of Pooh," I said.
"What's the Tao of Pooh?"
"You know—the Uncarved Block, The Cottleston Pie Principle, the Pooh Way, *That* Sort of Bear, and all that."
"Oh," said Pooh.
"That's the Tao of Pooh," I said.
"Oh," said Pooh.
"How would *you* describe it?" I asked.
"Well . . . this just came to me," he said. "I'll sing it to you."
"All right."
"Now, then . . . (*erhum*),"

To know the Way,
We <u>go</u> the Way;
We <u>do</u> the Way
The way we do
The things we do.
It's all there in front of you,
But if you try too hard to see it,
You'll only become Confused.
I am me,
And you are you,
As you can see;
But when you do
The things that <u>you</u> can do,
You will find the Way,
And the Way will follow you.

"That's what I think it is," he said.
"*Perfect*," I said. "But you know, don't you. . ."
"Know what?" said Pooh.
"It's the same thing."
"Oh," said Pooh. "So it is."

From *The Tao of Pooh* by Benjamin Hoff, 1982.

137

Smokey the Bear

A famous and much-loved creature in the United States is Smokey the Bear. He is popular not only because he is so helpful and friendly, but also because he symbolizes the need to prevent the careless destruction of our forests through fire.

In 1950, the Lincoln National Park in New Mexico was ravaged by a violent forest fire—the origin of the disaster, a careless camper. While trying to

From The Bear in the Burning Forest, by Jane Werner, 1956. Illustrated by Richard Scarry.

extinguish the fire, the firefighters found a small bear cub that had saved itself by climbing up into the top of a tall tree. At first, the cub was named Hotfoot Teddy, but it soon began to be called Smokey the Bear in memory of the smoke-filled surroundings in which it had been found. Smokey the Bear was given a new home in the zoo in Washington, D.C., and was adopted by the U.S. Department of Agriculture as a symbol of the fight against forest fires.

In 1953, the Ideal Toy Corporation was given permission by the Department to manufacture a toy bear to be called Smokey the Bear. Everyone who bought this bear then became a Junior Forest Ranger. Smokey the Bear is a clever aid when it comes to teaching children to be careful with fire in wooded areas.

Since Smokey the Bear started being used as a symbol, the number of forest fires has been sharply reduced. On innumerable posters and stickers, his characteristic figure in his broad-brimmed hat warns campers and travelers about prudence with fire. In children's books and comics, he plays a major role. His familiar visage has even appeared on a U.S. stamp. Apart from his hat, his chief characteristic is his spade, the kind firefighters use for flattening smoking ground fires.

138

The work of the American poet Gary Snyder has deep roots in Buddhist teaching with its respect for all living things. Mr. Snyder studied and practiced Zen Buddhism in Japan, where he lived for several years; but he is also highly practical in a very American way. As a student, he supported himself by working during the summers as a forest ranger and National Park guide. Close to his home in northern California he has built a small Zen Buddhist temple, and there he and a group of like-minded people meditate and sing sutras.

Gary Snyder can be both humorous and profound. When he transforms Smokey the forest ranger into Buddhist divinity, he provides a source for laughter as well as for contemplation. (On suitable occasions, Mr. Snyder himself has been known to don Smokey's wide-brimmed hat).

Smokey the Bear Sutra

Once in the Jurassic, about 150 million years ago, the Great Sun Buddha in the corner of the Infinite Void gave a great Discourse to all the assembled elements and energies: to the standing beings, the walking beings, the flying beings, and the sitting beings—even grasses, to the number of thirteen billion, each one born from a seed, were assembled there: a Discourse concerning Enlightenment on the planet Earth.

"In some future time, there will be a continent called America. It will have great centers of power called such as Pyramid Lake, Walden Pond, Mt. Ranier, Big Sur, Everglades, and so forth; and powerful nerves and channels such as Columbia River, Mississippi River, and Grand Canyon. The human race in that era will get into troubles all over its head, and practically wreck everything in spite of its own strong intelligent Buddha-nature."

"The twisting strata of the great mountains and the pulsings of great volcanoes are my love burning deep in the earth. My obstinate compassion is schist and basalt and granite, to be mountains, to bring down the rain. In that future American Era I shall enter a new form: to cure the world of loveless knowledge that seeks with blind hunger, and mindless rage eating food that will not fill it."

And he showed himself in his true form of

SMOKEY THE BEAR

A handsome smokey-colored brown bear standing on his hind legs, showing that he is aroused and watchful.

139

Bearing in his right paw the Shovel that digs to the truth beneath appearances; cuts the roots of useless attachments, and flings damp sand on the fires of greed and war;

His left paw in the mudra of Comradely Display—indicating that all creatures have the full right to live to their limits and that deer, rabbits, chipmunks, snakes, dandelions, and lizards all grow in the realm of the Dharma;

Wearing the blue work overalls symbolic of slaves and laborers, the countless men oppressed by a civilization that claims to save but only destroys;

Wearing the broad-brimmed hat of the West, symbolic of the forces that guard the Wilderness, which is the Natural State of the Dharma and the True Path of man on earth; all true paths lead through mountains—

With a halo of smoke and flame behind, the forest fires of the kali-yuga, fires caused by the stupidity of those who think things can be gained and lost whereas in truth all is contained vast and free in the Blue Sky and Green Earth of One Mind;

Round-bellied to show his kind nature and that the great earth has food enough for everyone who loves her and trusts her;

Trampling underfoot wasteful freeways and needless suburbs; smashing the worms of capitalism and totalitarianism;

Indicating the Task: his followers, becoming free of cars, houses, canned food, universities, and shoes, master the Three Mysteries of their own Body, Speech, and Mind; and fearlessly chop down the rotten trees and prune out the sick limbs of this country America and then burn the leftover trash.

Wrathful but Calm, Austere but Comic, Smokey the Bear will illuminate those who would help him; but for those who would hinder or slander him,

HE WILL PUT THEM OUT.

Illustrator: Michael Corr, 1973.

140

Thus his great Mantra:

Namah samanta vajranam chanda maharoshana

Sphataya hum traka ham mam

"I DEDICATE MYSELF TO THE UNIVERSAL

DIAMOND

BE THIS RAGING FURY DESTROYED"

And he will protect those who love woods and rivers, Gods and animals, hobos and madmen, prisoners and sick people, musicians, playful women, and hopeful children;

And if anyone is threatened by advertising, air pollution, or the police, they should chant SMOKEY THE BEAR'S WAR SPELL;

DROWN THEIR BUTTS

CRUSH THEIR BUTTS

DROWN THEIR BUTTS

CRUSH THEIR BUTTS

And SMOKEY THE BEAR will surely appear to put the enemy out with his vajra-shovel.

Now those who recite this Sutra and then try to put it in practice will accumulate merit as countless as the sands of Arizona and Nevada,

Will help save the planet Earth from total oil slick,

Will enter the age of harmony of man and nature,

Will win the tender love and caresses of men, women, and beasts

Will always have ripe blackberries to eat and a sunny spot under a pine tree to sit at,

AND IN THE END WILL WIN HIGHEST PERFECT ENLIGHTENMENT.

thus have we heard.

Smokey the Bear Sutra by Gary Snyder, 1973

Bears of Fable

From Book of Fables
for Young People by
Franz Hoffman, 1873.
Illustrated by Karl
Offerdinger.

fables had been part of the oral tradition for about five hundred years.

The European animal fables are short tales with a few animals as main characters. The animals speak and think like people and have very definite characters. The most common animal is the fox. But although only a dozen or so fables are about bears, these are nevertheless among the most popular. Perhaps this is because the bear combined tremendous strength with childish credulity.

In the world of fables, the fox is cunning and crafty, while the wolf is cruel and ruthless. The bear is certainly strong, but often easily deceived and stupid. Occasionally, however, a word of wisdom also comes from the bear's mouth. In one fable, two friends meet a bear in the forest. One man flees and the other throws himself down and pretends to be dead. The bear goes up to him and whispers in his ear that he should watch out for friends who leave him in the lurch at the first opportunity. Then the bear lopes off without harming the man.

Whatever happens in the fable, everyone has to watch out for the bear. All the other animals are frightened of his mighty strength and anger. But the cunning fox often exploits the bear's strength to his own advantage, as in the tale about the bear and the fox who went threshing. On other occasions, the fox plays on the bear's credulity, as in the following story about how the bear got his stumpy tail.

The animal fable is a very old popular folk story; the oldest was written down in Greece in about 300 B.C. European books of fables were first printed in the early seventeenth century, but before that,

Primary School Children's
Newspaper (Sweden). No. 35.
Kerstin Frykstrand, 1933

How the Bear got his Stumpy Tail

Long, long ago, when the bear still had a long tail, he one day met the cunning Michael Fox, who was carrying a fish he had stolen from a fisherman.

The bear would have liked a meal of fish. So he asked Michael how he had got the fish. The fox then said he had sat by a hole in the ice and fished it up with his tail.

The bear at once ran down to the ice and sat down on the edge of the hole. Patiently, he sat there all night with his tail in the water, waiting and waiting to catch a fish.

In the morning, he thought he could feel a bite on his tail. Quickly, he tried to jerk it out, but it had frozen fast in the ice and broke off. From that day to this, the bear goes around with nothing but a stump of a tail.

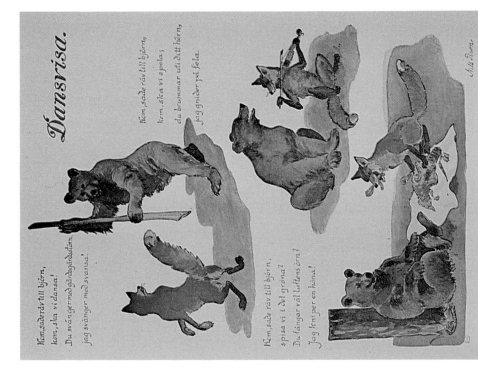

Dansvisa.

Kom, sade räv till björn,
kom, ska vi dansa!
Du svänger med gårdagskjärn,
jag svänger med svansa!

Kom, sade räv till björn,
kom, ska vi spela;
du brummar uti ditt horn,
jag gnider på fela.

Kom, sade räv till björn,
spisa vi i det gröna?
Du fångar väl i aftons örn?
Jag hint per en häna!

Nils Gren

When the Bear and the Fox Went Threshing

The bear and the fox were to go threshing.

"Now let's see who's best at threshing," said the fox.

Of course, the bear wanted to be the best. He thumped and threshed away, so the fox didn't have to do anything.

Then they were to share the corn.

"You can have the biggest heap," said the fox.

The bear was quite satisfied with that division. So the bear had the largest heap, which consisted of the husks, and the fox had the threshed corn.

"My corn," said the bear, "is so gray and ugly, while yours is fine and clean."

"Yes," said the fox. "That's why it's so fine and clean. You do that, too!"

So the bear went off and threw his corn into the river, where it all floated away, while the fox picked up his heap and went home.

From Fables from Mora, 1928.

Strong as a Bear, Soft as a Teddy Bear

Few animals have been used so diligently in advertising as the bear. Since it exists as both a wild animal and a domestic teddy bear, it gives rise to a great many associations. The fact that the toy bear is treated as a member of the family—that is, as a human being—also plays a large part in our perception of bears and teddy bears.

In the Service of Man

In Europe and America the bear has been featured in advertising since the middle of the nineteenth century. A Swedish company that has used a bear as their trademark for almost a hundred years is Barnängen. On their trademark, a bear sits grinding away at some substance in a mortar. The mortar and pestle are associated with pharmaceutical goods and the chemical industry, but what has that to do with bears? It seems that the property on which Barnängen's factory in Stockholm was located included at one time a small zoo, created by the founder of the factory, Johan Wilhelm Holmström. Among other animals, he kept live bears there in cages. Naturally, they did not help crush the shells used for the

144

manufacture of tooth powders, but on the company trademark, the bear was eminently suitable as an image of power and strength.

The bear is drawn as a real bear, yet it sits like a human being and works with a tool. The bear as a trademark lends the impressions of great strength and effectiveness. The bear using the mortar has kept his shape over the years, but the trademark is seldom used nowadays on products or packs. It is still found in relief in Barnängen soap and on the lid of Bear Glue jars. Previously, Barnängen used teddy bears and bears a great deal in their advertisements—in particular, with the goods intended for children.

So in Barnängen's trademark, the wild bear has been taken out of its natural surroundings and has become an aid to human beings. Many other companies use the bear in the same way.

I'm a Talking Telephone!

K.C. BEARIFONE II™

"My mouth and eye movements 'lip-synch' a caller's voice! I'm a 2-way speakerphone (no handset is needed) who makes every phone conversation a fun event!"

"For fun, watch my eyes and mouth move, synchronized to every word said by anyone with whom you are having a phone conversation!"

"But don't overlook the fact I'm a real working telephone! A push-button dial hands-free speakerphone that lets you Converse at a distance, without a handset."

A QUALITY TELEPHONE BY
TeleConcepts INC
NEWINGTON, CT 06111

In the United States, Behr-Manning, a manufacturer of sandpaper, used the association with both the company's name and the bear's power to devise a logo with a simple, realistic bear standing erect inside a triangle. "Barney," as the bear was affectionately dubbed, was also used in advertising designed to appeal to children as well as to their parents. The campaign offered the smiling Barney as a stand-up cut-out, with a variety of costumes: deep sea diver, farmer, photographer, baseball player, and so on.

Building Supply, Inc. uses a friendly teddy-like bear, lying on a slab of lumber as it watches a bee circling over a jar of honey. The effect is pleasing, though it is difficult to say exactly what message was intended: nature's resources in the service of humans, perhaps?

The *White Bear* soap powder that Helios started selling in the 1920s has a

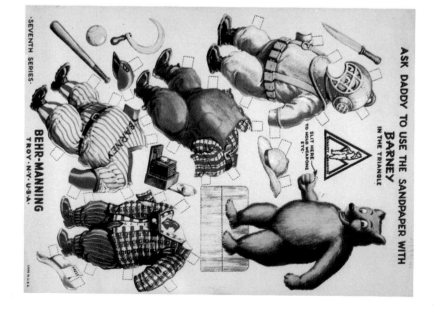

polar bear as its symbol. The polar bear adds its whiteness to the white soap powder and white wash. On advertisements and billboards, the bear is shown smiling broadly and invitingly. It polishes, scrubs, and cleans—an image of the true homemaker or servant.

A similar quick and industrious bear can be found in the advertisement for *Red Bear* polish, which cleans copper, brass, and stainless steel. On older cans the bear is portrayed full face, standing on all fours with the characteristic toss of the head. In recent years, this bear has been exchanged for a more stylized bear on two legs, wearing an apron and holding a polishing rag and a copper pan in his paws. In other words, the bear has become a person—a helper in the household.

It is one short step from the concept of the bear as a household helper to the use of the bear as a practical, if fanciful, household object. The bear's love of honey has led to the widespread use of

This Hungarian bear waiter is serving his own box of cheese. Above his right arm is the older trademark with a realistic bear on four legs.

...lastic honey bottles—usually in the shape of a sitting bear. Much more fanciful is the "Bearifone," a telephone encased in a teddy bear whose eye and mouth movement synchronize with the caller's voice.

Teddy Bear, the Lover of Sweets

Several ice cream companies use the bear as their symbol, with polar bears being especially suitable. The *Teddy Bear Ices* advertisement figure is extremely stylized, with a wavy outline indicating fur, a pointed, upturned nose, and a licking tongue. It only faintly resembles a polar bear.

The Danish *Premier Ice* bear takes on a slightly different form. It is a very sylized bear that walks on all fours. The firm has created a round and amusing figure, and done away with the real polar bear's pointed nose and long neck. *Premier Ice's*

freestanding advertising figure in plastic looks like a toy bear.

Although the polar bear lives mainly on flesh and fish, other bears consume fruit, berries and other sweet things. Advertisements and product labels, like that for Little Rhine Bear Liebfraumilch, highlight these tastes. In fact, not only do

bears eat sweet things, but they themselves are eaten, in the shape of candies and cookies.

Cracker Jacks, the sweetened popcorn confection, was quick to associate the

bear's sweet tooth with President Theodore Roosevelt and Teddy, his popular namesake. The "Cracker Jack Bears" series featured smiling animals dressed in striped coats and polka-dotted trousers shaking hands with President Roosevelt in a variety of locations. Here, the steps of the Capitol are transformed into a circus, with a second bear watching from the middle of a column as he prepares to launch himself on a trapeze.

Caught in Bear Yarn

The strength of the bear can also stand for durability. *Bear Brand Thread*—yes, indeed, that sounds strong! The English firm of J. and P. Coats knew what it was doing when it included a bear in its trademark on its spools of cotton thread. As in so many trademarks in the past, the

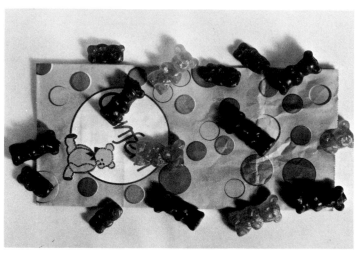

148

suit the women who were to buy Bear Brand's stockings. The dangerous bear was changed into a happy little teddy bear named Chad, after the town of Chad Valley in which the factory was located. Suavely attired in a bow tie and top hat, and carrying a cane, Chad invites the women to go out and enjoy themselves—strength has lost out to elegance.

The gallant cavalier Chad lends a risqué undertone to the stocking advertisement. In other contexts, the erotic allusion is clearer. In a German ad for *Triumph* underclothes, a giant teddy bear—or a man in a teddy costume—has captured inside a hoop a beautiful woman wearing only a vest and panties. She is holding the teddy's head against her cheek and is kissing his nose. The message is that the undergarments are as soft and

The "Cracker Jack Bears" No 7.

Coats bear is very like a real bear. *Teddy Bear Wool's* nice Winnie-the-Pooh-like bear sitting there knitting is, on the other hand, somewhat distant from the reality of any animal. Teddy Bear Wool is not only selling its durability and quality, but also implying its softness and showing how pleasant it is to knit with.

At times, the emphasis on the bear's strength fades into the background, as can be clearly seen in the evolution of the trademark of *Bear Brand* nylon stockings. This American firm originally had a grizzly bear as its symbol—its nylon stockings were thus represented as strong and indestructible. But the image of the grizzly was too savage and uncivilized to

something beyond softness and warmth is being alluded to here.

In the saga, the girl kisses a wild animal and finds a prince. In folklore, women are captured by bears and made to spend the winter in their caves. The bear stands for passion as a force of nature. When the bear in the advertisement becomes a teddy bear, sexuality receives a more suitable form for society.

nice as a teddy bear. But the picture also offers other associations. Why does such a big girl need a teddy bear? Clearly,

Omega and the Bear, Edvard Munch, 1902. "One day she met the bear; Omega trembled when she felt the bear's soft fur against her body; when she put her arm round his neck, it vanished."

can be placed differently. In modern ads, the powerful shoulders have vanished, the detail that emphasizes strength. Stylization can go so far that the bear is given completely circular forms.

In the symbol for the *World Wildlife Fund* with its black-and-white panda, those circular and nice-to-hug forms in particular have been emphasized. There are other animals threatened with extinction that could have been used as a symbol and a challenge to deserving contributions. But it is easy to empathize with a cute little round panda with an appealing and slightly melancholy expression in its eyes and touching turned-in paws. Who is equally tempted to hug a golden eagle or a rhinoceros? In reality, a bear's eyes are rather small and really look more malicious than anything else. But in the ads the teddy bear's eyes are large and kind with a look that goes straight to our hearts.

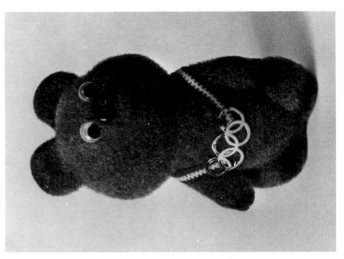

Nice and Round

In 1900 the Pettijohn company used a full grown bear as its trademark. This realistic symbol of strength contrasts sharply with the playful, humanized cubs that are being frightened by an angry cat. Meanwhile, Mama, in skirts and cap, dashes to the rescue of her little ones. Thus, humor and charm predominate, and the company's original, powerful image literally fades into the background.

In today's society, the bear and nature are put in their respective places. In both ads and other contexts, everything frightening is avoided. Instead, ad creators appeal to the human being's need for tenderness and security. Thus, the teddy bear of childhood and the feelings it arouses become a usable symbol.

With its great, heavy shape, the bear is easy to stylize and so also easy to reproduce. Its high shoulders and hump, its big backside, its little head, and its turned-in toes—all are features that can be exploited. Also, the center of gravity

The Russian bear is often portrayed as large and menacing, but in the 1980 Winter Olympic Games held in Moscow, it assumed the appealing form of little Mischa, the symbol of those games. That popular round little figure became known all over the world. In the form of badges, toys, ornaments, and other souvenir items, it was bought by people of many countries and races, and served to offer a positive attitude to the Soviet Union.

The teddy bear has more and more become a symbol for children and childhood in general. In Sweden, the Road Safety Department issued a brochure in 1985 about safety inside the car. A girl is sitting on the back seat with her safety belt fastened and a large teddy bear beside her. The teddy reinforces the sense of security, both as a familiar toy and as a father-figure as well. The *We Parents* society issues a sticker that also urges safety for children in the car. On it the child has been replaced by a teddy bear with his safety belt fastened. The picture of the bear tells us at once that the information concerns children.

In the United States an increasing number of police and fire departments are now carrying teddy bears as standard equipment in their vehicles. When the officers encounter a frightened or injured child, they present him or her with a cuddly teddy. "Bear Buddies," as some of the local companies have named the program, has proven invaluable in comforting traumatized children.

Thus, in advertisements and in public service campaigns the bear of the forest has become increasingly the teddy bear of toyland. It no longer represents the savage and untameable, but has become a safe and helpful friend.

Bibliography

Teddy Bears

Bull, Peter. *A Hug of Teddy Bears*. New York: E.P. Dutton, 1984
Hillier, Mary. *Teddy Bears: A Celebration*. Methuen, 1985
Schoonmaker, Patricia N. *A Collector's History of the Teddy Bear*. Maryland: Hobby House Press, 1981
Waring, Philippa and Peter. *Teddy Bears*. London: Treasure House, 1984

Making Your Own Teddy Bear

Hutchings, Margaret. *Teddy Bears and How to Make Them*. New York: Dover, 1964
Jacksier, Barbara and Ruth. *Crocheting Teddy Bears*. New York: Dover, 1984
Michaud, Terry and Doris. *How to Make and Sell Quality Teddy Bears*. Cumberland, Maryland: Hobby House Press, Inc., 1986
Moore, Marsha Evans. *The Teddy Bear Book*. New York: Allen D. Bragdon Publishers, Inc., 1984
Worrell, Estelle Ansley. *Classic Teddy Bear Designs*. Cumberland, Maryland: Hobby House Press, Inc., 1986

Bears and Bear Hunting

Ormond, Clyde. *Bear!* Harrisburg, Pennsylvania: The Stackpole Company, 1961
Roosevelt, Theodore. *American Bears, Selections from the Writings of Theodore Roosevelt*, ed. Paul Schullery. Boulder, Colo.: Colorado Associated University Press, 1983
Waterman, Charles F. *Hunting in America*. New York: Holt, Rinehart and Winston, 1973

Political Cartoons

Mullins, Linda. *The Teddy Bear Men: Theodore Roosevelt and Clifford Berryman*. Maryland: Hobby House Press

Picture Credits

Amherst Teddy Bear Rally, Amherst, MA 145d
Ingvar Andersson 19a
Anders Backlund/Kristian Königsson/Erik Ronne 100, 101, 102, 103a, b
Eva-Lena Bengtsson 145b, c
Christer Berglund 29c, 149b
Carl Erik Bergold 62a
Bibliothèque Nationale, Paris 56c, 76a
Culver Pictures 71a, 149a
Birgitta Ögvall 147d
Jarl Högbom 43a
Mats Jonell 27b
Olle Lindman 8a, 10, 13, 15b, 16a, b, d, 19b, 20d, 21a, 22b, 23, 26, 27b, 28, 29a, b, d, e, 34, 53b, 86, 98b, 103c, 106, 107, 110b, 111, 114, 115, 116c, 117, 144a, 148b, 151a, d, 154, 155
Jack Mikrut 153
Nationalmuseum 53a, 55b, 63a
Nordiska Museet 64
Olof Norling 97b
Hans Odöö 45
Peter Dominic Ltd 147a
Postmuseum 20c
Pressens Bild AB 61b
Anders Qvarnström 6
Joan Roberts 146a
Maj Rudberg 22a
Patricia Schoonmaker, *Collectors History of Teddy Bears*; *Teddy Bear and Friends Magazine*; Hobby House Press, Cumberland, MD 17, 95b, 150c
Rolf Segerstedt 9
Upplandsmuseet 7
Karin Svedlund 98a
Teleconcepts 145a
Daniel Werkmëster 116b, 148c
Jerk-Olof Werkmäster 128b
Niklas Werkmäster 21c
Öffentliche Kunstsamlung, Basel 56a